D1257528

Memphis:
1800-1900

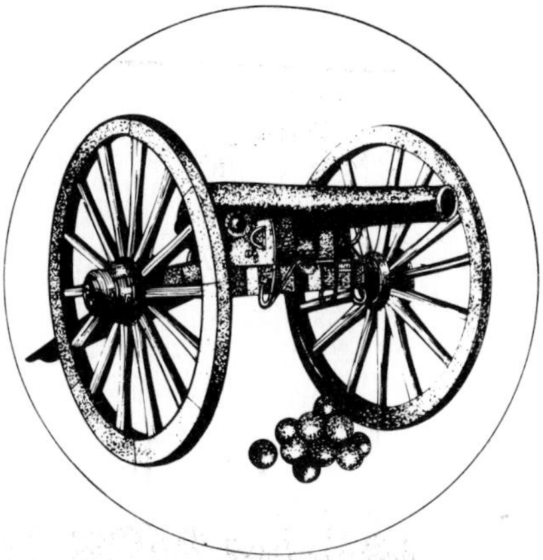

Volume II: Years of Crisis 1860-1870

Memphis

1800–1900

Volume II · Years of Crisis · 1860-1870

BY
FREDRICK LEE COULTER

EDITED BY
JOAN HASSELL

A Memphis Pink Palace Museum Book
PUBLISHED BY
NANCY POWERS & COMPANY PUBLISHERS, INC.
NEW YORK

Published by Nancy Powers & Company Publishers, Inc.
241 Central Park West, New York, New York 10024

LIBRARY OF CONGRESS CATALOGING IN PUBLICATION DATA

Ornelas-Struve, Carole M., 1941 – Memphis, 1800–1900.

"A Memphis Pink Palace Museum book."
Bibliography: p. 121.
Contents: v. 1. Years of Challenge, 1800–1860
v. 2. Years of Crisis, 1860–1870
v. 3. Years of Courage, 1870–1900.
1. Memphis (Tenn.) – History. [1. Memphis (Tenn.) – History]
I. Coulter, Fredrick Lee, 1945.
II. Hassell, Joan.
III. Memphis Pink Palace Museum. IV. Title.
F444.M557076 976.8'19 81-17920
AACR2
(Set) ISBN 0-941684-03-2
(Volume 2) ISBN 0-941684-01-6

The drawings created especially for this book
were rendered by Daphne F. Hewett

Photographs by William J. Cupo, Jr.

First Printing

Designer: Helen Barrow
Printed in the United States of America
1 2 3 4 5 6 7 8 9 10

Preface

This book is a direct outgrowth of the production of a major, permanent exhibit dealing with 19th century Memphis and the Mid-South region, developed over a seven year period, at the Mempis Pink Palace Museum. The majority of photographs, illustrations and other materials are a part of this important exhibition. The thousands of hours involved in researching the script, writing and developing label copy as well as participating in design efforts made the production of a series of books paralleling the exhibit a compelling need.

It is not necessary to view the more than 2,500 artifacts on exhibit at the Pink Palace to enjoy this narrative history. By the same token, enjoyment of the exhibit is not dependent on the purchase of the book series; each stands on its own merits.

The history of Memphis is well worth telling. Each of us who has been involved with the development of the exhibit and the book believes this series takes a somewhat different approach in bringing the exciting and often turbulent 19th century in the Mississippi Valley to life. We hope you will read and enjoy this volume and, if possible, see what should be counted among the very finest museum exhibit installations dealing with the history of a city and a region.

DOUGLAS R. NOBLE
DIRECTOR OF MUSEUMS

Acknowledgments

MANY PEOPLE have contributed significantly to this three volume Museum Series. It is my hope as author that I do not fail to give each of them appropriate recognition in this acknowledgment.

Let me begin by thanking the President, Gus B. Denton, and the members of the Board of Trustees of the Memphis Pink Palace Museum Foundation, Inc. The financial support of these civic-minded individuals is responsible for making this project a reality.

This book would not have been possible without the efforts of these members of the Memphis Pink Palace Museum's staff: Lou Adair, Edna Bomar, Ronald C. Brister, Carole M. Ornelas-Struve, Meredith Pritchartt, Marilyn Van Eynde, and the special assistance of Museum Director, Douglas R. Noble.

Special research consultants were Dr. John Harkins, Eleanor McKay and Sue Olsen.

Finally, I am indebted to the West Tennessee Historical Society, the Mississippi Valley Collection of Memphis State University, and the Memphis and Shelby County Library and Archives for their contributions.

FREDRICK L. COULTER

Contents

Introduction

THE PURPOSE of each of the three volumes of *Memphis 1800–1900* is to provide the public with a cultural history of the 19th century Lower Mississippi Valley that is informative and easily understood.

Every chapter consists of numerous illustrations accompanied by a descriptive narrative which offers insight into the lives of those who lived there during the 19th century: what they cooked and cultivated and made and bought; what they wore; the houses they lived in and the furnishings they used; how they were educated, entertained or travelled; the ways they worshipped; and all the small, seemingly unimportant things of which ordinary daily life is comprised.

It is the story of a people who came from many nations and experienced boom times and hard times. Many were people who rose from log cabins to grand mansions only to have their prosperity swept away in the chaotic conflict that split a nation. Undaunted, they began repairing their lives and fortunes only to be struck down once more by a death that reached into every home and filled the dead wagons which rolled through the city of Memphis. They refused to be defeated and responded each time with a stubborn courage that made them indomitable.

Anyone who treasures family anecdotes or heirlooms that once belonged to a grandparent or a great-grandparent will enjoy this intimate portrait of the formative years of this important region.

Memphis 1800–1900 is an inspiring story and a tribute to the rich and poor, the clever and uninspired, the slave and soldier and all the thousands of people who were a part of the *Years of Challenge, Years of Crisis* and *Years of Courage.* The story of 19th century Memphis is their story.

THE EDITOR

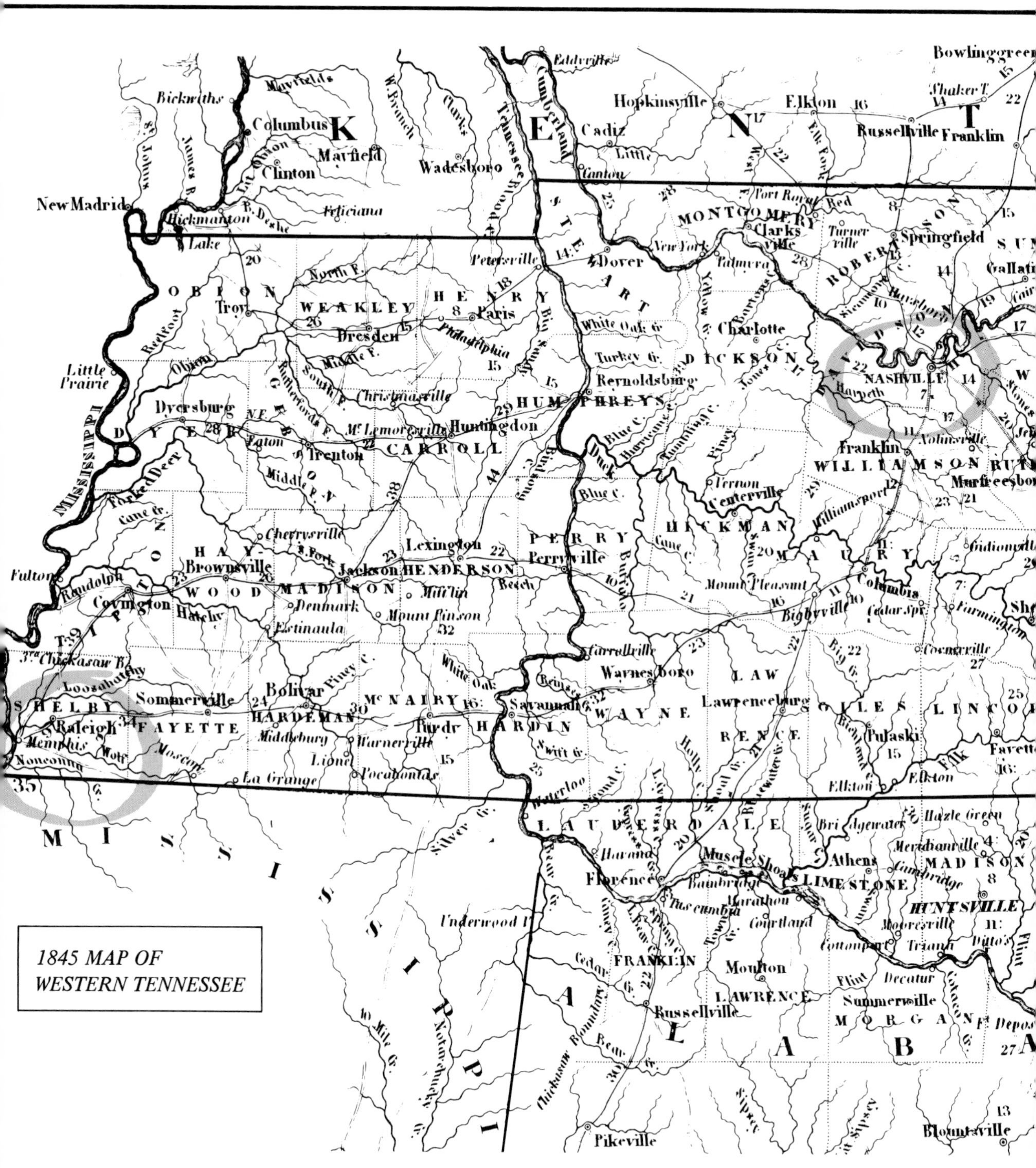

1845 MAP OF
WESTERN TENNESSEE

Early power-driven cotton gin.

CHAPTER 1

The House Is Divided

JACKSON BUST
Rebel Memphians would soon make this inscription a target for their hatred of the Union.

TO SALVOS of cannon on the bluff, brightly uniformed marchers, blaring bands, a cheering crowd and Masonic ceremonies, a marble bust of Andrew Jackson was unveiled in Court Square on January 8, 1859, the anniversary of the Battle of New Orleans. Forty years after John Overton, James Winchester and Andrew Jackson founded the town of Memphis, the citizens paid tribute to one of them. On the north side of the pedestal supporting the bust were carved Jackson's famous words:

> THE FEDERAL UNION: IT MUST AND SHALL BE PRESERVED.

Two and a half years from that day, sectional emotionalism would cause Memphians to turn from the preservation of the Union to its destruction.

One of the local dignitaries attending this ceremony was the six-foot, two-inch, 38-year-old alderman, Nathan Bedford Forrest. Still largely unknown outside his own state, Forrest's name, like Abraham Lincoln's, would soon be written in large letters on the pages of Civil War history.

Forrest was a man of pioneer stock, self-educated and with little formal schooling. Unlike Lincoln, who

ALDERMAN FORREST
Nathan Bedford Forrest was elected to three terms as alderman by the citizens of Memphis prior to the Civil War.

had once been an unsuccessful Illinois storekeeper, Forrest had demonstrated marked commercial acumen early in life and the ability to overcome great obstacles.

When his blacksmith father died, Bedford, as his family and friends called him, was 16 and became the head of a family of eight boys and three girls. Before he was 21, this youth had not only improved the family's financial condition but provided educational opportunities for the younger children as well.

By 1851, when Forrest came to Memphis, he had already acquired a small fortune in livestock trading. In Memphis he became a dealer in livestock, real estate and

THE COTTON LEVEE
This scene on the Memphis bluff above the steamboat landing was sketched before the war by an artist for the national illustrated magazine Harper's Weekly. *At the left is a cotton buyer with large scales for weighing cotton bales and coming up from the river with freight is a mule-drawn two-wheeled dray. Just beyond are ox-drawn freight wagons and the covered wagons of westward-bound pioneers.*

slaves and remained in these activities until 1859, when he sold his lucrative slave mart and became a cotton planter in northern Mississippi. He and his wife, Mary Ann, and their son, Willie, could now live among their fellow Memphians without the slave dealer's social stigma. On the eve of the Civil War, his plantation was producing a thousand bales annually, and Forrest was among the millionaires being multiplied by the wave of prosperity in Memphis.

From the tiny settlement of 50 people in 1820, Memphis had grown to over 20,000 people and was being boosted by enthusiastic promoters as the fastest growing

city in the United States, the "Chicago of the Lower West." Within the past decade Memphis had become a major commercial and transportation center for the Middle South, with over $53 million being transacted annually by cotton traders, wholesalers, manufacturers and those involved in river and rail traffic.

Four railroads now converged at the bluff, among them the Memphis & Charleston, which had linked the city with the Atlantic seacoast in 1857. Hundreds of steamboats stopped at the river landing to carry the over $16 million worth of cotton shipped each year. In recent years the crews of telegraph company president Henry Montgomery had strung direct telegraph lines to Nashville, New Orleans, Little Rock, Arkansas and Tuscumbia, Alabama, which connected Memphis with the major cities in the Northeast and with England by 1858. In August of that year Memphis' pride was reflected in the message sent to Manchester, England, over the newly installed "trans-Atlantic" cable.

"The City of Memphis on the shore of the Mississippi, the largest interior depot of cotton in America, sends her greetings to the city of Manchester, the largest manufacturing city of that staple in Great Britain and desires to mingle her congratulations with those of her trans-Atlantic sister upon the successful establishment of the ocean telegraph."

Communication with the far West also improved when the first completely overland mail in the United States left Memphis September 16, 1858, and arrived in San Francisco 24 days later on a coach of John Butterfield's Overland Mail Company.

Three- and four-story structures now lined the river bluff on each side of the imposing Exchange Building, which housed city hall and other public and private offices. Commercial buildings were going up by the block in the central business district: the Irvin Block (future Confederate hospital and Federal prison) located at Second and Court; the Overton or Brinkley Block (which would become the Peabody Hotel in 1869) at Main and Monroe; and other structures which now crowded the Memphis skyline. On Monroe Street the Bruce brothers erected the first five-story brick building in the city to house their carriage factory. The Greenlaw brothers, building contractors for Robertson Topp's elegant Gayoso House, the finest hotel in the city, had recently completed New Orleans style market houses on Poplar and on Beale. Seventy-two years later the Beale Street site would become Handy Park.

Property values shot up to phenomenal heights as a

MEMPHIS SKYLINE CIRCA 1858
Antebellum Memphis was a prosperous and busy river port as well as a major transportation center for the Middle South. This Harper's Weekly *illustration shows a large number of impressive structures along the bluff and steamboats lined up at the river landing as side-wheelers, a raft and a keelboat move past in midstream.*

GOVERNOR ISHAM G. HARRIS
Memphian Isham Harris was governor when Tennessee seceded from the Union and retained that title throughout the Civil War. When Tennessee came under Union control, however, Lincoln appointed Andrew Johnson military governor.

ANTONIO VACCARO
Vaccaro, one of the early European immigrants to Memphis, was the founder of a family which has made significant contributions to the culture and commerce of the city for generations.

result of the building boom. A parcel of land worth $20 in 1850 was selling for ten times that much only five years later. Within one decade the taxable wealth of the city had risen almost 500 percent—from $4,600,000 to $21,500,000 for an 1860 population of 22,623.

Among the men contributing to this greater affluence were financier Robert Brinkley, development entrepreneur and railroad president Robertson Topp, merchant Frederick Cossitt, carriage maker Amos Woodruff and cotton merchant Wardlow Howard. Among the Memphians who had become prominent in both the public and private sectors were Senator James C. Jones and Tennessee's governor, Isham G. Harris. More names were added to these ranks each year as Memphians prospered and new merchants and professional men arrived to open a store or an office. Memphis had as yet an unstratified society, and individuals could move up the economic ladder to heights of wealth by their own industry and enterprise, unhindered by their origins.

Irish schoolmaster Eugene Magevney turned his teaching fees into profitable investments and then put his immigrant brothers, brothers-in-law and nephews on the same path toward prosperity. In 1844 another immigrant, a 20-year-old Italian from Genoa named Antonio Vaccaro, had walked off the gangplank of Captain "Charley" Church's steamboat and soon had his own confectionery, fruit and cigar store on the northeast corner of Jefferson and Front Streets. Stimulated by his success, Vaccaro encouraged other Italians to come to Memphis and start businesses. With the outbreak of the Civil War, some of these would join other Italian-born Memphians in forming the Garibaldi Guards to fight for the South.

Joseph Clouston, Memphis barber, ex-slave and pioneer land-owning black, had taxable assets of $650 in 1850; ten years later his assets were valued at $20,000. He owned several pieces of land, including a lot on Beale Street purchased in 1851, giving him the distinction of being the first of his race to own property on Beale.

Clouston was one of 198 free blacks living in Memphis on the eve of the Civil War. They worked as butchers, blacksmiths, draymen (freight carriers), public hack (taxi) drivers, bricklayers, carpenters, seamstresses, bakers, steamboat stewards, maids, firemen or stevedores. The one trade almost exclusively the province of the free black was barbering or hair dressing. It proved lucrative not only for Clouston but for others, such as Thomas Williamson, who was able to purchase his manumission with proceeds from his after-hours barbering on a Mason, Tennessee, plantation. Shortly after setting himself up in business in Memphis, the industrious and talented Williamson earned enough to buy his mother's freedom.

Free blacks were only a fractional part of a pre-war, multiracial and multinational community whose ethnic diversity produced a cosmopolitan culture. While 17 percent of the 1860 Memphis population was black,

CHILDREN OF IMMIGRANTS
These children reflect the diverse origins of antebellum immigrants to Memphis. The young girl is wearing what appears to be a Middle European native dress, and the baby's tartan sash suggests parents of Scottish nationality.

ANTEBELLUM LADY
Verandas and hoopskirts were the trademark of the antebellum era of affluence in Memphis.

about 36 percent, or roughly one out of every three whites, was foreign-born. The largest national group among these were the Irish (4,159), with the Germans in second place (1,412), followed by the English, French, Scots and others. Many of the foreign-born were middle-class tradesmen and craftsmen whose livelihood was derived from supplying the economic elite who lived in the fine homes and elegant antebellum mansions lining residential thoroughfares such as Adams, Jefferson, Beale and Vance.

Here lived the Robert Brinkleys, the Amos Woodruffs, the Robertson Topps, and the William R. Hunts in a rarified atmosphere of luxury and elegance. In large dining rooms with frescoed ceilings, wainscoted walnut walls and heavy sideboards gleaming with an array of silver, 25 or more guests were provided multicourse banquets. Entrees and side dishes were served on the finest English or Bavarian china and accompanied by sparkling crystal goblets of chilled vintage wines from the select stock of the B. J. Semmes Company. Meals were climaxed by elaborate confections and capped by the men with fine brandy and Havana cigars before they joined the ladies in the parlor or salon. There they were entertained by a display of the keyboard and vocal virtuosity of a daughter of the house or a talented female guest.

Music lessons for the daughters were provided by Professor Winkler on pianos purchased from H. M. Grosvenor with sheet music sold by E. A. Benson. The

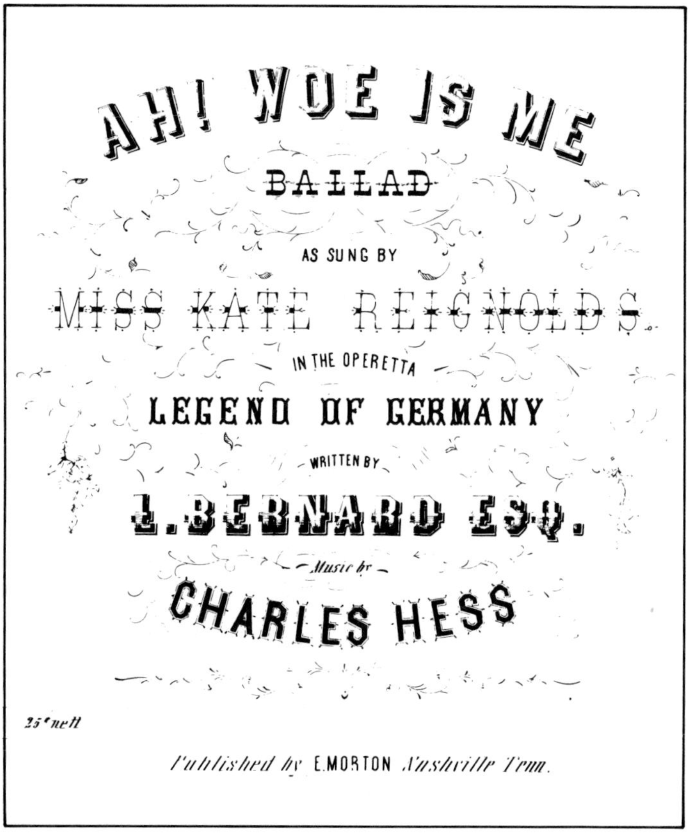

PRE-WAR SHEET MUSIC
Sentimental ballads such as this one appealed to young people in the years that preceded the Civil War. (Mississippi Valley Collection)

young lady's musical accomplishments were sometimes displayed on romantic evenings when her favorite beau was permitted to turn the pages of the latest sentimental ballad.

Above the mantles, in heavy gilt frames, were hung oil portraits of the head of the house, painted by local artists such as James Hart. Those of lesser means often had their stiff, unsmiling portraits made in the photographic studio of "daguerrean artist" Y. A. Carr.

In addition to the legitimate entertainment offered in the city, the young sons of the elite found additional diversion in saloons, gambling houses and impromptu racing matches on Main Street. These "speeding" activities earned the censure of those who complained the police arrested draymen trotting at a fast pace but not the young scions of the wealthy.

Unlike many of these sons and daughters of affluent families, 18-year-old Kate Magevney was the product of a strict Irish Catholic upbringing that was turning her older sister, Mary, toward religion. Eugene Magevney wanted his girls schooled by the church and sent them to St. Mary of the Springs Convent in Ohio.

The man who would one day capture Kate's eye and heart was John Dawson, a close friend of her cousin Michael, or "Modus" as he was called by the family to distinguish him from his uncle Michael. Both John and the younger Michael were fire-eating secessionists and were among the many youths who filled the ranks of the nine military companies formed in the city since 1852.

In spite of the martial airs of these strutting youths, parading in colorful uniforms to the cheers of their hoopskirted sweethearts and the sometimes heated words between opposing political factions, a comfortable complacency wrapped most citizens in a cotton-lined cocoon of political indifference, economic self-interest and materialistic self-indulgence that was soon to prove the city's downfall.

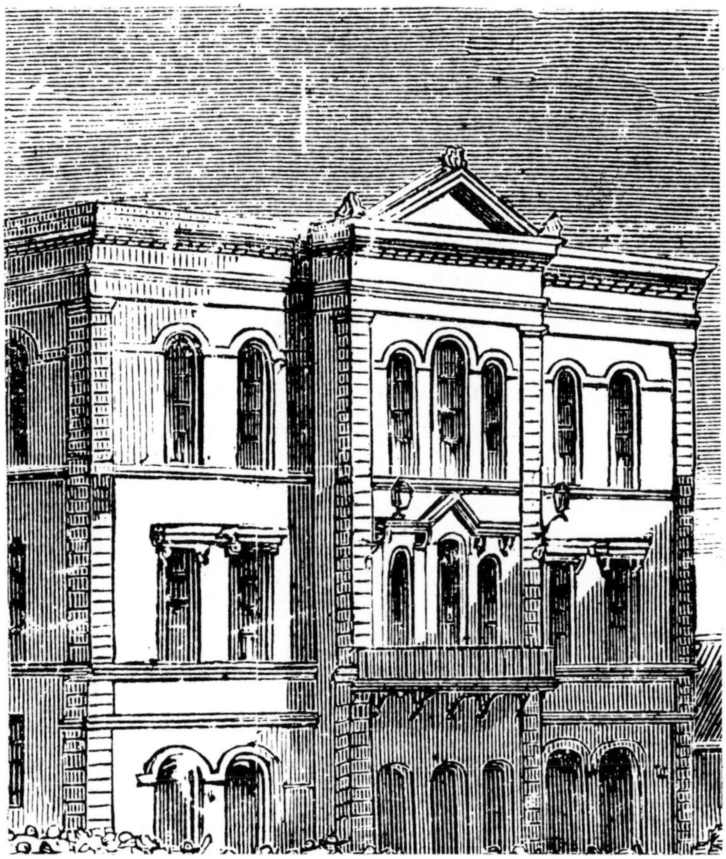

NEW MEMPHIS THEATRE
Originally called Crisp's Gaiety Theatre, this lavishly decorated building on Jefferson east of Third Street was constructed in 1857 at a cost of over $40,000. During the winter social season, Memphians could see leading dramatic artists such as Shakespearean actor Edwin Booth (brother of John Wilkes Booth, Lincoln's assassin) in classical productions.

Memphis by 1860 had six newspapers, nine new banks, 21 churches, three female seminaries or colleges, two medical colleges, 21 public schools, two orphanages, a city hospital, public horsecar transit and gas lights on some streets and in some homes. The city could also boast of its 1,000-seat New Memphis Theatre where Edwin Booth and other stars performed nightly during the season. There were also the Hightower and Odd Fellows Halls for lectures, concerts and minstrel shows, along with a philharmonic society and a jockey club which sponsored high-stake races in the spring and fall.

In spite of Memphis' progress in commercial ventures, the administration of the city was marked with a bungling ineptness. The city still had boggy streets into which every layer of gravel vanished under the busy wagon traffic. Other signs of governmental neglect included a jail and workhouse that Alderman O'Mahoney described as "loathsome and horrible, not fit for a good dog to lie in," and leaky public cisterns, the result of a failure to establish a public water works.

Although the wharf along the riverfront had finally been paved with cobblestones, it had cost the taxpayers $40,000 instead of the original bid of $17,000. The labor of chain gangs, which was profitable for most cities, cost Memphians $20,000 a year, partly because it took a captain and two overseers to supervise the work of only one or two prisoners. According to Alderman Robinson it would have been cheaper to shut "the prisoners up in the calaboose." There were whispers of graft, but nothing was ever proved. A committee appointed by the board of aldermen found "the (city's) books in satisfactory condition," but reported "there was a great want of system in various departments, and great facilities existed for fraud."

MATT GALLAWAY
Editor and founder of the antebellum Memphis newspaper, the Avalanche, *Gallaway conducted a violent verbal battle with the* Appeal *during the 1860 presidential election.*

In spite of this report and the reform zeal of newly elected aldermen Robinson and O'Mahoney or the reelection cleanup promises of Mayor Richard Baugh, the same inertia continued to affect administrative activity. Disgusted with the constant bickering and indecision which crippled effective action, Alderman Bedford Forrest submitted his resignation on August 10, 1860. John Park and Eugene Magevney's brother, Michael, refused the offer to replace the popular Forrest, and his seat was finally filled by Judge Selby.

As summer changed into fall, local political problems were being replaced in parlor discussions by concern over the possible ramifications of the coming Presidential election. The pro-Union *Appeal* tried to allay the electorate's fears about the Republican Party's candidate saying, "There is nothing to be apprehended from the election of Lincoln," and went on to point out that "any civil commotion arising south of us" would bene-

APPEAL—EVENING EDITION.

BY M'CLANAHAN & DILL. MEMPHIS, MARCH 22, 1862. OFFICE---UNION STREET.

EVENING APPEAL.

A FALSE PROPHECY.—The New York *Herald* gives its opinion of the immediate consequences of the war. From the quotation given below it will be seen what Bennett is hoping for:

Here is what the same paper thinks, or professes to think, will be one of the immediate consequences of the war:

We think it very probable that one of the immediate consequences of this war will be an emancipation pressure upon the border slave States, which will rapidly operate to the abolition of slavery therein; and by the action of these States themselves, in view of the changed condition of things around them, Maryland, Virginia, Tennessee, Kentucky, and Missouri, with the restoration of the Union, will, we think, find it to their advantage to slough off the institution of slavery as quickly as possible, consistently with public tranquility. We think, too, that such will be the course of said States, with the issue in their hands; and the question should be left to them, and to every other slave State of the present day, as it was left originally to [illegible] Pennsylvania, and others. This is the policy of "Honest Abe Lincoln;" and as it has been consistently pursued in the reclamation of Maryland, Missouri, Kentucky and Tennessee from the gripe of this rebellion, we may venture the opinion that it will still be adhered to, all the emancipation schemes of Sumner, Trumbull, Lovejoy, Cheever, Beecher and Greeley to the contrary notwithstanding.

BOGUS MILITARY CHARACTERS.—We see by our Richmond exchanges that since the declaration of martial law there, a number of bogus military characters who, since the beginning of the war, had been curvetting on fiery steeds, dressed *cap a pie* in gray uniforms and hussar caps, have been arrested and imprisoned. Alluding to the matter, the *Examiner* says:

Besides the fraud they are practicing on the public, these popinjay civilians are doing mischief by increasing the difficulties of detecting deserters from the army. Henceforth every man in uniform will be treated as a soldier, and will be required to show his papers. It is well.

OLD BEN WADE.—The Cincinnati Enquirer is rather severe on Ben. Wade as follows:

AN UNCONDITIONAL UNION MAN.—The principal candidate before the unconditional Union Legislature of Ohio for United States Senator is Benj. F. Wade. To show what an unconditional Union man Wade is, we publish the following extract from a speech which he made at Portland, Maine, in 1856. Wade said:

"There was really no union between the North

Interesting European Intelligence.

Papers and correspondence by the Arabia furnish the following:

Forty-five Spanish war vessels are to sail for the Pacific in April. They are to rendezvous first at Montevideo, and then start for other parts of the American coast.

Prince Napoleon made an important speech in the French Senate on the liberty of the press, and in defense of the government. He said the empire signified to him the glory of France abroad, the destruction of the treaties of 1815, and the unity of Italy. The empire has but "one justification, and that is when it becomes an application of the principles of the revolution."

The Papal government was removing a portion of the sacred archives from Rome.

The *Gazette de Cologne* observes: At his last audience with his holiness, the following significant words struck upon the Marquis de Lavalette's startled ear: "We are thinking of repairing to Vienna, when we can no longer remain here with our full dignity." The Marquis is reported to have exclaimed in alarm, "Surely, Holy Father, you would not occasion a universal war;" to which no answer was returned.

At Rome an attempt has been made upon the life of the Marquis de Lavalette. The assassins, who all belong to the Legitimist party—one being a Belgian, the second a Bavarian, and the third a Neapolitan—have all been arrested, and will be tried by a French military tribunal. The Marquis was not injured.

The Paris correspondent of the London *Herald*, February 14th, says:

The American exodus still continues. The timorous return to the States, and the wealthy, who are not afraid their fortunes will greatly suffer by home events, take contrary route to Rome. A piece of news last night was transmitted to me by a southerner, which should not be omitted. The person alluded to received by the latest mail a letter from a young friend, in which it stated that he had applied to Gen. McClellan for a passport in order to proceed to Richmond. The General at once granted it. But when it was presented to Mr. Seward, he refused to countersign it, giving as his reason for not doing so that he expected in the course of three weeks every one who pleased would be free as formerly to leave and enter Richmond.

The Paris correspondent of the New York *Herald*, after stating the stagnation of business throughout France was deplorable, says:

The masses are frightened, and, as usual with the French when they become so, they also become cruel. Now they snarl and sneer at the *entourage* of the Emperor, speak of the millions swallowed up by those persons, and hint at a day of reckoning. I tell you the time is fast approaching when the government must strike some grand *coup* if it wishes to avoid the fate of its predecessors.

The great idea now seems to be an intervention in favor of the South. I can assure you

The Fremont Expose.

[From the New York Express, March 6.]

We,—not "Lincoln men," never in "the Lincoln green"—cannot but be delighted with Gen. Fremont, because of that renewed insubordination of his, which withdraws his purported defense of himself from the war committee of Congress, and prints it, in a *Tribune* extra. Lookers-on—[illegible] of mischief, all, must thank him, heartily thank him, for his exposes. The *private* letters which he publishes of P. M. G. Montgomery Blair are rich, racy, rollicking, even:

"Chase—writes Blair (P. M. G.)—has more horror of seeing treasury notes below par than of seeing soldiers killed, and therefore has held back too much, I think."

Racy, Mr. Blair!

"I showed the President Billing's letter, and him yours about Adams. He said that you were right in saying that Adams was devoted to his money-bags."

Who is Money-bag Adams?

"The main difficulty is, however, with Lincoln himself. He is of the Whig school, and that brings him naturally not only to incline to the [illegible] policy of Whigs, but to give his confidence to such advisers. It costs me a great deal of labor to get anything done, because of the [illegible] of mind on the part of the President, and leading members of the Cabinet, including Chase, who never voted a Democratic ticket in his life."

Rich as well as racy, Mr. Blair.

But now, look here, and read the following, marked 'private,' from the President, which his major-general has not the least hesitancy in ushering into print:

THE PRESIDENT TO FREMONT.

[Private.] WASHINGTON, D. C.,
September 2, 1861.

To Major-General Fremont:

MY DEAR SIR: Two points in your proclamation of August 30, give me some anxiety.

1. Should you shoot a man, according to your proclamation, the Confederates would very certainly shoot our best men in their hands, in retaliation; and so, man for man, indefinitely. It is, therefore, my order that you allow no man to be shot under the proclamation, without first having my approbation or consent.

2. I think that the closing paragraph, in relation to the confiscation of property, and the liberating slaves of traitorous owners, will alarm our Southern Union friends, and turn them against us—perhaps ruin our rather fair prospect for Kentucky. Allow me, therefore, to ask that you will, as of your own motion, modify that paragraph so as to conform to the first and fourth sections of the act of Congress "an act to confiscate property used for insurrectionary purposes," approved August 6, 1861, and a copy of which act I herewith send you. This letter is written in a spirit of caution, and not of censure. I send it by a special messenger, in order that it may certainly and speedily reach you.

Yours, very truly, A. LINCOLN.

Letter from Decatur.

[From the New Orleans Picayune.]

DECATUR, Ala., March 14.—Two gentlemen arrived here to-day from Nashville report that the Federal generals are becoming more stringent and insolent toward the citizens. Miss Saunders, daughter of Mrs. A. V. Brown, had been called on by Gen. McCook, who sent him word that she could not receive him as she was in mourning for her country. The Rev. G. C. Harris, an Episcopal clergyman, had been arrested and brought before Gen. McCook, for using the prayer for the Congressional President of the Confederate States, McCook insisting that no Episcopal clergyman had a right to use any other prayer than that for the "United States." Mr. Harris asked if it was the intention of the Federal army to interfere with the prayers of the church. McCook replied, "Yes sir, I shall." Mr. Harris was then permitted to depart.

A balloon and apparatus had arrived at Nashville for making observations of our army. Also, a signal guard of forty men, for the purpose of giving information at distant points to their army. Six or eight transports went up the Cumberland last Tuesday, supposed to be on a foraging expedition. Three ferry boats were running across the Cumberland. Andy Johnson has arrived at Nashville. The small pox is reported to have broken out among the Federal troops at Clarksville. The citizens of that place are not permitted to leave their houses after 8 o'clock P. M.

Bells.

Our fair correspondent, "A Lady," is right in saying that copper and tin are necessary to make gun-metal, called brass. The parts for the alloy is about as ten of copper to one of tin. The best brass is four of copper to one of tin.

The best bell metal is about four parts of copper to one of tin—eighty parts of the former in a hundred to twenty of the latter. So that bell metal is just the very thing to make cannon of.

Brass cannon is not now in use for heavy ordnance. It is mostly confined to moveable field pieces. For this kind of artillery it is considered superior to iron.

What the component parts of candle sticks and brass stair rods, etc., are, we cannot say; but we suppose that with bell metal they will form a good amalgam for the purpose.

Bells are sometimes made of a composition of copper, tin, zinc and lead. Zinc is used in small bells in order to give them a shrill sound.

So we think that the people had better contribute their brass to help General Beauregard. He has called for it, and no doubt, of whatever composition it may be, he will find means to put it to the service of his country.

Yesterday, we received two small contributions: the one was brought to us by a handsome bright little fellow who was too young to tell us his name. He was four or five years of age, and bore with him an armfull of stair-rods. The other was a contribution from Mrs. Mathews—bells, candle-sticks, etc., with a small amount of

APPEAL, *MARCH 1862*
Strongly pro-Union in 1860, the Appeal *became an ardent supporter of the Southern cause after the fall of Fort Sumter. When Memphis surrendered, it began a vagabond existence, printing Confederate news until its press was captured in the last months of the war.*

fit Memphis in both "wealth and population." The prosecessionist *Avalanche*, edited by the fire-breathing Mississippian Matt Gallaway, responded with anti-Lincoln editorials dipped in brimstone.

Memphians voted for candidates opposing Lincoln that November election day; however, they still voted 8 to 1 for preserving the Union by voting for pro-Union Democrats. While Lincoln did not get their votes, he did not need them; Abe swept the field clean with a clear majority of 180 electoral votes against 123 divided among the three major opposing candidates—Douglas, Breckinridge and Bell.

Confirmation of Lincoln's election sent the South Carolina legislature into special session, and on December 20, 1860, it formally "dissolved (its) union with the United States of America." The federal structure had been fractured.

The South Carolina legislature also elected a new governor, Francis W. Pickens, a former congressman and U.S. Minister to Russia. (In 1858, before accepting the Russian post, Pickens had married Lucy Holcombe, the daughter of a wealthy La Grange, Tennessee, planter. While the winds of sectional strife were stirring in their

LUCY HOLCOMBE PICKENS
This belle from a wealthy and cultured La Grange, Tennessee family became famous throughout the Confederacy.

home states, the young couple were becoming such close friends of Czar Alexander II that their first child, a daughter, was born in the royal family's Winter Palace with the Czar and Czarina serving as godparents.)

By February 1, 1861, all the other states of the lower South had followed South Carolina's lead. Virginia, Tennessee, North Carolina and Arkansas did not leave the Union at this time but announced their intention to secede if the Federal government attempted to use force against any of the seceded states. Tennesseans wavered, torn between loyalty to the flag of their fathers and loyalty to their Southern brethren. Although the odds were changing, Memphians still rejected secession by a 4-to-3 vote in February.

The first month of 1861 witnessed nightly torchlight rallies and parades by pro- and anti-Union supporters while the *Avalanche* and *Appeal* fought a war of words in print. The pro-Union vote in February was largely due to the statewide efforts of men like Robertson Topp, Minor Meriwether, William R. Moore and other pro-Union conservatives, who were supported by a large number of foreign-born citizens, especially Germans.

Minor Meriwether, a civil engineer for Memphis railroads, not only spoke at rallies in the city but also stumped the state in support of the Union. The eldest son of Garrett Meriwether, a Kentucky plantation owner who disliked slavery, Minor completed his father's manumission plans for the plantation's slaves upon Garrett's death. Emigration by the freed blacks, who were educated for missionary work in Africa or relocation in a state north of the Ohio River, was financed by the young Meriwether, who sold the plantation and then resumed his engineering studies. Like many other Southerners who opposed both slavery and secession, Meriwether and his family were soon caught up in events beyond their control as emotions replaced rational thought.

On February 8, 1861, the Confederate States of

America were formed at Montgomery, Alabama, with Jefferson Davis as provisional president. Ten days later Memphis bandmaster Herman Frank Arnold conducted his new arrangement of "Dixie" for the inauguration of the Confederacy's first and only president. A week later a "Memphis Secession Directory" was published by the *Avalanche.* It contained more than 800 names of those endorsing secession and "no concession of Southern rights."

Secession and war fever hit Memphis in full force in April. Memphis merchants unanimously voted on April 2, 1861, to join the Confederacy whether the rest of Tennessee joined them or not. In the middle of April came the final blow to any hope of preserving national unity. Fort Sumter surrendered to Confederate forces, and President Lincoln issued a national call for 75,000

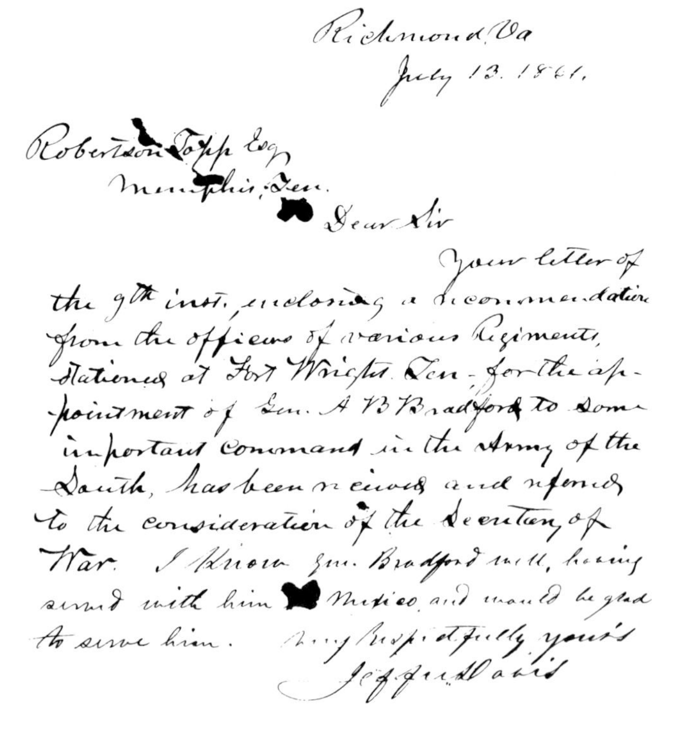
Richmond Va
July 13. 1861.

Robertson Topp Esq
Memphis, Ten.
Dear Sir
Your letter of the 9th inst. enclosing a recommendation from the officers of various Regiments, stationed at Fort Wright Ten. for the appointment of Gen. A B Bradford to some important command in the Army of the South, has been received and referred to the consideration of the Secretary of War. I know Gen. Bradford well, having served with him Mexico and would be glad to serve him. Very Respectfully yours
Jeffn. Davis

JEFFERSON DAVIS' LETTER TO ROBERTSON TOPP
Like many other influential leaders in the South, the former pro-Union Robertson Topp gave wholehearted support to the Confederacy after the fall of Fort Sumter. The Fort Wright mentioned in the letter was one of several fortifications above Memphis built by the Confederates in 1861 to protect the lower river ports. Fort Wright was located just north of Fort Pillow and the First Chickasaw Bluff.

(TRANSCRIPTION OF LETTER)

Dear Sir

Your letter of the 9th inst. enclosing a recommendation from the officers of various Regiments stationed at Fort Wright, Ten. for the appointment of Gen. A. B. Bradford to some important command in the army of the South, has been received and referred to the consideration of the Secretary of War. I know Mr. Bradford well, having served with him in Mexico and would be glad to serve him.

Very Respectfully Yours
Jeffn. Davis (Confederate President)

MINIATURE CONFEDERATE FLAG
Memphian Frederick G. Gutherz, a member of the 154th Senior Tennessee Infantry Regiment, carried this pocket-sized flag throughout his Civil War service. The flag is eight and one-half inches by 18 inches and has 12 white stars on a dark blue background with two red stripes and one white stripe. Several flag factories in Memphis were making all sizes of Confederate flags early in 1861.

troops to put down the rebellion. The news of Sumter's fall was celebrated by wildly cheering crowds and a boisterous meeting of 3,000 Memphians defiantly voting for secession. Even the formerly pro-Union newspaper, the *Appeal*, switched its allegiance and joined its one-time opponent, the *Avalanche*, in ardent support of the Southern cause.

On June 8, 1861, in spite of last-ditch efforts of East Tennessee Unionists led by "Parson" William Brownlow's *Knoxville Whig*, Tennessee became the 11th and last state to join the Confederacy. The line was now drawn between 11 states with a population of nine million and 23 states with a population of 22 million. Even without the industrial might of the North, the odds were weighed heavily against the South. Only a war of short duration or a foreign alliance could bring success to the Confederacy.

The strategic importance of Memphis was evident. It was the northern gateway to the Mississippi River Valley, the transportation center for the Middle South and the

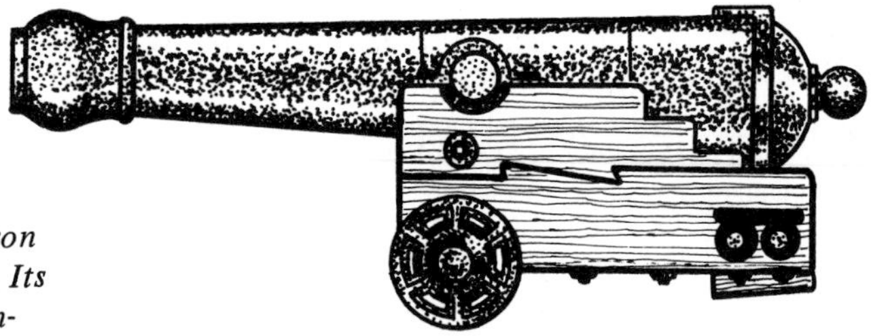

32-POUNDER CANNON
This smoothbore cannon, which fired 32-pound iron balls, was used in early Confederate fortifications. Its inability to penetrate the iron-plated armor of gunboats left river forts virtually defenseless and made all such cannon obsolete as weapons.

largest cotton depot in the nation. For this reason, when news came of a Federal force organizing at Cairo, Illinois, the riverfront was hurriedly barricaded with a wall of cotton bales, and the city voted $59,000 for defense.

The Confederacy also came to the aid of Memphis. The Confederate Congress ordered General Gideon Pillow to supervise construction of a chain of fortifications along the Mississippi River between Memphis and the Kentucky border and appropriated $125,000 for two gunboats to protect the city. These would become the Confederate rams *Arkansas* and *Tennessee.* From Little Rock came four cannon, from New Orleans, a battery of 32-pounder cannon, and from Mississippi, 3,000 muskets and a half-million rounds of ammunition.

Factories began converting from peacetime products to those of war. As early as May the Quinby & Robinson Foundry, located at the foot of Poplar Street on the riverfront, began casting cannon and manufacturing munitions while cannonballs were being made in the Memphis & Charleston Railroad shop. Factories were organized to make gun carriages and cartridges. At the paper cartridge factory where 55 men and 230 women worked, a bonus for increased production boosted output to 75,000 paper cartridges daily while the men molded 2,000 pounds of lead into musket balls each day.

Memphis had become a vast military camp as young men flocked to the colorfully named volunteer companies, such as the Emerald Guards, the Shelby Grays,

$2,000.00

No. 263

FOUR PER CENT. PER ANNUM.

In pursuance of the authority conferred upon the Secretary of the Treasury by the seventh section of the act of Congress entitled "An act to reduce the currency and to authorize a new issue of notes and bonds," approved February 17th, 1864, the Confederate States have borrowed from

TWO THOUSAND DOLLARS,

payable on demand. The said sum to bear interest at the rate of FOUR PER CENT. PER ANNUM from date indorsed hereon until paid. And to secure the same, an amount of bonds issued in conformity with the sixth section of said act, equal to the said sum, is hereby hypothecated.

In Witness Whereof the Register of the Treasury, in pursuance of the said act of Congress, hath hereunto set his hand and affixed the seal of the Treasury, at Richmond, the 29 day of Aug 1864.

Entered

Recorded

REGISTER

CONFEDERATE BOND

Financing the war was a major concern of the Confederate government throughout its existence. By 1864 the Confederate treasury was in such poor condition the government called in all currency notes over $5 for conversion into bonds, payable in 20 years.

WESTERN FOUNDRY
AND
ENGINE MANUFACTORY,
North side of Center Landing, fronting Exch'ge Building.

S. B. CURTIS & A. G. KNAPP,
ARE PREPARED TO MAKE TO ORDER
STEAM ENGINES
Complete, embracing Cast, Wrought and Sheet-Iron Work.
***Also*—Copper and Brass Work;**
Cast Iron Water Wheels, and all
MILL MACHINERY,
Made in the most perfect and durable manner.
GIN GEAR,
Of the best Patterns always on hand, and warranted to wash well. Also—a New
Portable Horse Power,
Suitable for all Plantation purposes,
Together with all other articles commonly kept in such Establishments.
S. B. CURTIS & Co.

QUINBY-ROBINSON FOUNDRY

Quinby-Robinson, the former Western Foundry, cast bronze 24-pounder field howitzers and 3-inch rifled cannon tubes for the Confederacy until the fall of Memphis.

the Crockett Rangers, the Memphis Light Dragoons or the Jeff Davis Invincibles. More than 50 of these companies of between 80 and 100 volunteers entered Confederate service from Memphis before the war's end.

The 154th Volunteer Regiment of the former Tennessee militia was placed under the command of Colonel Preston Smith of Memphis. In these ranks were Kate Magevney's future husband, John Dawson, and her cousin Michael. By the war's end the 154th had fought in some of the fiercest battles of the war and its commanders were Colonel Michael Magevney and Lieutenant Colonel John Dawson.

Among the older recruits was the former alderman Nathan Bedford Forrest, a private in the ranks of the Mounted Tennessee Rifles. Another enlistee was Minor

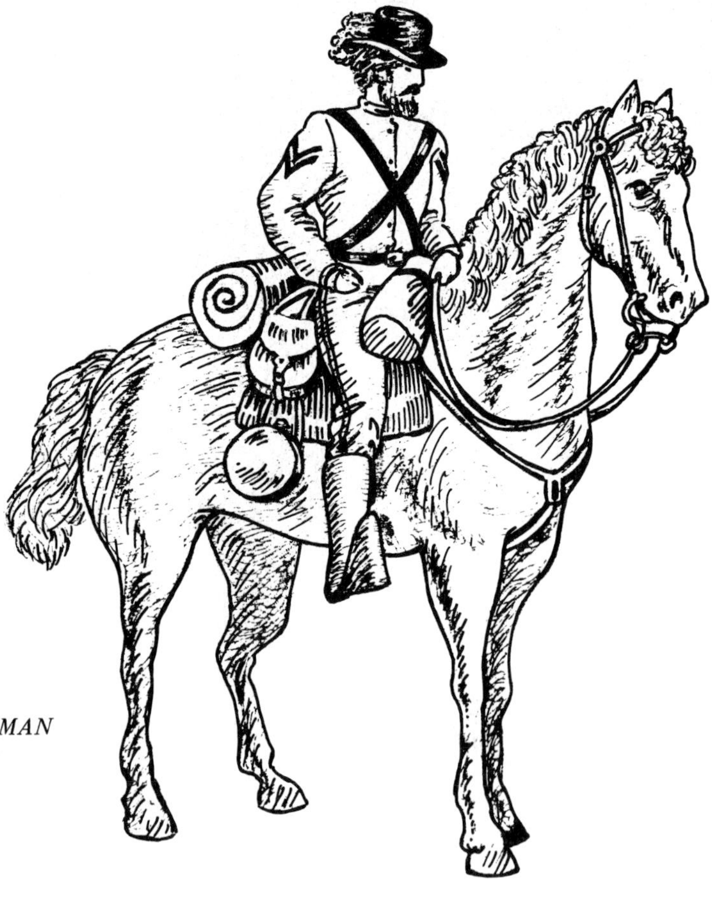

CIVIL WAR CAVALRYMAN

GINGER BEER BOTTLES
Non-alcholic ginger beer was a popular beverage bottled in stoneware containers like these.

Meriwether, whose final loyalty was to his own state. He was commissioned an officer of engineers and would build bridges for the Confederate army until the war was over.

The city provided men for the Confederacy but could not properly equip them. This problem faced General Leonidas Polk, the "soldier bishop," when he set up his headquarters in Memphis for the Confederate Western Department in July 1861. His captain of ordnance was Memphian William Richardson Hunt, who worked desperately to assemble arms, ammunition and war materials. In August Captain Hunt wrote these prophetic words to General Polk:

"If this war should unfortunately be prolonged, the valley of the Mississippi must ultimately become its great theater, for the enemy now working to subjugate the South knows the value of our great artery of commerce and of the prominent cities upon it too well for us to doubt that he will bend all his energies to control them."

Although there were shortages of war materials, there was no reason for any Confederate in Memphis to

GAYOSO HOUSE
This famous hotel on Front Street served as military headquarters for Confederate Generals Pillow and Polk. After the fall of Memphis, high-ranking Union officers and civilians stayed here.

CIVIL WAR SERGEANT
(Mississippi Valley Collection)

go thirsty that first year of war. By August 31, 471 barrels of whiskey and wine by the barrel, cask, box and basket, had arrived in the city along with almost $11,000 worth of ale and beer. Also received was more ice (19,654 tons) than iron (2,827 tons), more limes and lemons than lead, and $400,000 worth of furniture. Memphians' taste for life's luxuries was as yet unstinted in those first months of war, but that soon began to change.

A small Missouri hamlet named Belmont, across the Mississippi River from Columbus, Kentucky, would bring the first lesson of war home to Memphians. On November 7, 1861, General Ulysses S. Grant steamed toward the Missouri shore with two gunboats and 3,000 troops to attack the Confederate regiments there, including the 154th and others containing Memphis companies. After a short and indecisive fight, resulting in a Confederate retreat and subsequent counterattack, Grant's force was driven back to the river. The stalemated battle produced more than 400 casualties in each of the opposing forces. Boats were sent up from Memphis to collect Confederate wounded, and anxious families crowded the bluff staring upstream until the boats began returning. The wounded were carried immediately to the hospital of the "Southern Mothers" in the Irvin(g) Block east of Court Square, the Catholic hospital of the Sisters of St. Agnes Academy and to many private homes.

Memphis had had its first taste of war, but not its last.

"QUEEN OF CONFEDERACY" BILLS

Lucy Holcombe Pickens, whose portrait appears on these Confederate $1 and $100 bills, was the only female so honored by the Southern government. Called the "Queen of the Confederacy," she was born in La Grange, Tennessee, in 1832 in a house which still stands. She married Francis W. Pickens, a young Congressman from South Carolina, who became Civil War governor of that state.

CHAPTER 2

Bugles, Bullets and Boredom

YOUNG OFFICER
Officers on both sides were often younger than the men they commanded. (Mississippi Valley Collection)

FEW OF the men who marched away behind the Bonnie Blue Flag of the Confederacy or the Stars and Stripes of the Union knew the first thing about war. Both sides were told by friends, sweethearts and old veterans that fighting for revered principles was a glorious thing.

Most of the combatants were young, between 18 and 30 years old, and had never fired a gun in anger. Some drummer boys were only 10 years old, and there were soldiers like Willie Forrest who were schoolboys barely in their teens. These youths naively saw war and the excitement of battle as an alternative to the drudgery of the classroom. One by one they had left John Milton Hubbard's male academy in Bolivar, Tennessee, to enlist. Finally even Professor Hubbard, a constant opponent of secession, closed his school and volunteered for service.

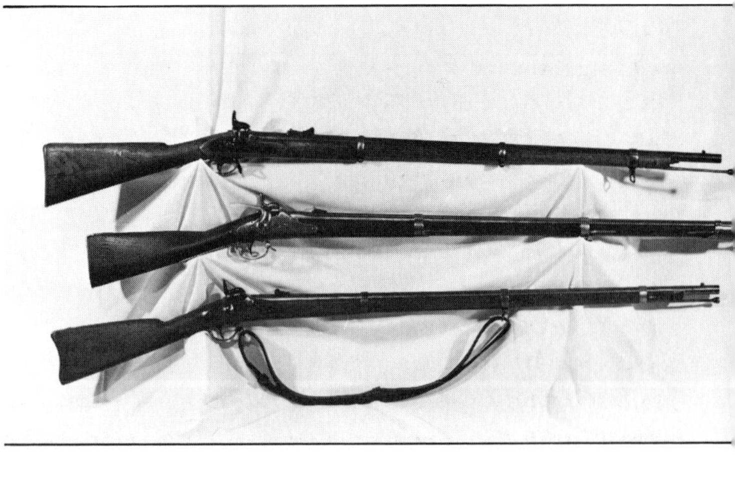

MUSKETS
The most common infantry weapon of the Civil War was a .58 caliber, muzzle-loaded rifled musket. Almost two million Northern muskets were made, and a half a million European muskets were imported by both sides. Top to bottom: British Enfield, U. S. Harper's Ferry, 1862 Springfield.

CARBINES
The carbine was a short, light weapon, well-suited to cavalry use since most were breechloaders and many were repeaters with a high rate of fire. Over 40 different models were in use during the war, with the eight-shot Spencer the most popular. Top to bottom: Spencer carbine, Burnside carbine, Sharp's carbine.

Not far from Jackson, Tennessee, was the farm of Alexander and Sallie Jones. Alex didn't enlist right away because he wouldn't leave his wife and their newborn child. However, when the baby was able to crawl, Alex left to become one of Forrest's troopers. In Illinois was another recruit, William Nicholas Fortune, whose wife, Lizzie, dreaded seeing her husband go off to war.

In each of the 34 once-united states there were mothers like Mariam Forrest Luxton who watched sons and grandsons go off to war. Enlisting soon after the fall of Fort Sumter were children of her first husband, William Forrest: Bedford, Jeffrey, William Jr., Jesse and Aaron; then two sons of her second marriage, to Joseph Luxton, volunteered; and finally her youngest, not quite 16, left to join the failing forces of the Confederacy. Only John Forrest, crippled and partially paralyzed by wounds from the Mexican War, did not serve the Confederacy. Throughout the nation there were thousands with a dearly loved sweetheart marching in ranks of blue or of gray, fathers who would outlive their sons and brothers who would never see each other again.

Few of the Southerners owned a slave, only one out of every five, so they fought not to preserve slavery but to protect their state's sovereignty, for which they were paid about 50 cents a day in inflated currency. They would survive for four years by capturing arms and ammunition, horses, food and almost everything else they needed from the Union army. Many clothed themselves with worn-out, patched militia jackets or re-dyed Yankee uniforms, or wore homemade jackets and pants of white and black wool mixed to give the fabric a grayish color.

Three and a half million men would serve the flags of the North and the South, and almost one million would die for one flag or the other. Out of the 1,100 men of Michael Magevney and John Dawson's regiment, the 154th Tennessee, fewer than 100 would be left when the South surrendered.

CONFEDERATE MONEY
Paper money backed by cotton or gold reserves was circulated by individual Southern states, towns and banks to pay for troops and war materials. Many of these notes became so worthless they were nicknamed "shinplasters."

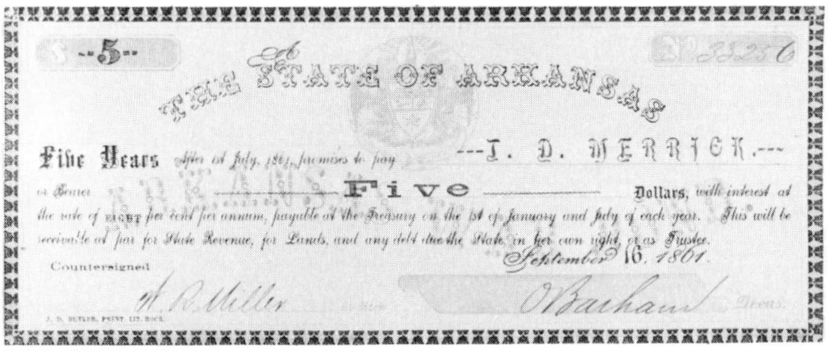

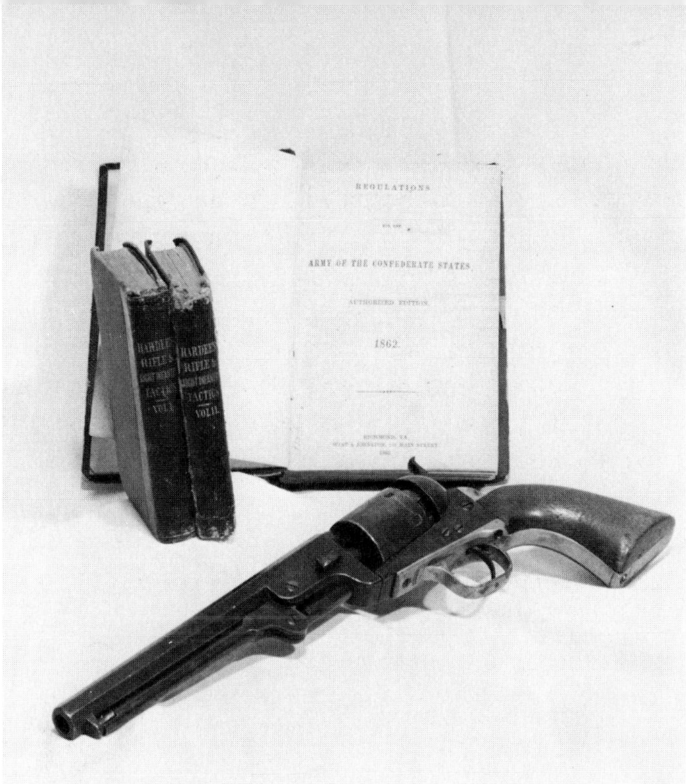

BOOKS AND REVOLVER
Newly commissioned officers spent more time in camp learning army regulations and drills or keeping their sidearms in top condition than they did leading troops in battle. The six-shot revolver is a colt navy, .36 caliber, 1851 model.

From that day near the end of May 1861, when General Pillow ordered all Memphis companies with 65 men or more to camp for training and Captain Magevney's Jackson Guards became Company F of the 154th Senior Tennessee Infantry Regiment, they all belonged to the army. Their lives would be dictated by military routine. A bugle, drum or officer would tell them when to get up, to go to roll call, to breakfast, to the doctor, to guard duty, to drill, to eat, to drill some more, to eat, to sleep, and when to get up the next day. As long as they were in camp, it was an unvarying schedule for six days of the week; only on Sunday were the men given a break in the routine.

When Captain White's company arrived at Camp "Yellowjacket," several miles north of Memphis at Randolph, Privates Bedford, Jeffrey and Willie Forrest of the Tennessee Mounted Rifles, now Company D of the 7th Tennessee Cavalry, soon learned what other raw recruits would discover in the course of the next four years—there was more boredom and bugles than bullets in a soldier's life. Over the space of a year even soldiers

LOADING A MUSKET
A paper or cloth cartridge was taken from the cartridge box on the belt and the powder end torn open with the teeth. The powder was then emptied down the barrel and the bullet pushed in with the thumb. The ramrod under the rifle barrel was detached and the cup-shaped end pressed against the bullet, ramming it down the barrel until the bullet was firmly seated on the powder.

in the most active regiment would typically be engaged in fewer than ten battles, none of which lasted longer than a couple of days, sometimes only a few hours. The rest of the seemingly endless days between were spent marching or waiting in camp for something to happen, anything to happen, just to give a break to the monotony of everyday routine.

At Camp "Yellowjacket" that break occurred even before army routine was established. The troops had to demolish a vicious force of stinging yellowjackets on the campsite. Soon after the winged enemy had been vanquished, Bedford was called to Memphis by Governor Isham Harris to recruit a battalion of mounted rangers and to become a Lieutenant Colonel. Not only would he recruit the companies for his future regiment, but he would also go to Kentucky and buy arms, saddles, harnesses and other equipment out of his own pocket and smuggle them back to Memphis.

In October Forrest and his men were ordered to report to Colonel Adolphus Heiman, commanding the 10th Tennessee (Irish) Regiment, then stationed at Fort Henry on the Tennessee River. Forrest's old regiment was sent from Randolph by steamer upriver to New Madrid, Missouri. The former Bolivar professor, now Private John Milton Hubbard, found this a pleasant change. "We really enjoyed camp life here as it was not so full of dull routine. A lively little scout or an amusing picket incident made our daily duties a little more spicy than usual."

Captain Magevney and Captain Dawson were sent with the rest of the 154th to various posts in Kentucky and Missouri, ending up in November in the village of Belmont, Missouri. Life there was not much different from that of Private Hubbard and his comrades until General Grant and 3,000 troops paid a surprise visit. After the wounded had been sent downstream on steamboats, the soldiers began bragging to each other, saying that they had "seen the monkey," which was army slang for being under fire.

TOILET KIT
Toothbrush, comb and hairbrush were stored compactly in a leather case that was easily carried in blanketroll or field pack.

Returning to the monotony of camp life, Captain John Dawson had to check the sick list and report on how many were returned to duty. He had to see that his men kept the area around their quarters clean and to be sure they had cut enough firewood for the cold days ahead. Dawson watched the guard details carefully to make sure no soldier stood his post longer than two hours out of every six and assigned extra drill to a sloppy platoon. These were only a few of the hundred small, routine duties in a line officer's life. It was tedious, boring work, brightened only by letters from home.

Letters, diaries, journals and notebooks helped the soldiers pass the time, and they supply a wealth of information on the everyday life of the common soldier dur-

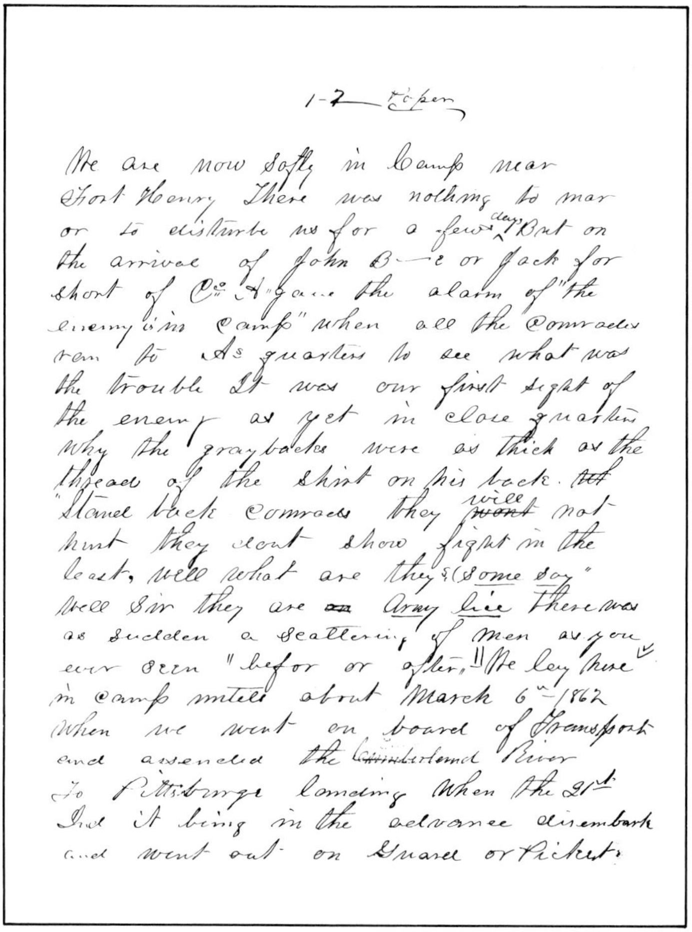

1-7 Copy

We are now safly in Camp near
Fort Henry There was nothing to mar
or to disturbe us for a few days But on
the arrival of John B—e or Jack for
short of Co "A" gave the alarm of "the
enemy is in Camp" when all the Comrades
ran to A's quarters to see what was
the trouble It was our first sight of
the enemy as yet in close quarters
Why the graybacks were as thick as the
thread of the shirt on his back. ~~tat~~
"Stand back Comrades they ~~wont~~ will not
hurt they dont show fight in the
least, well what are they" (some say"
Well Sir they are an Army lice there was
as sudden a scattering of men as you
ever seen "befor or after." We lay here
in camp untill about March 6th/1862
When we went on board of Transport
and assended the ~~Cumberland~~ Cumberland River
To Pittsburge landing When the 21st
Ind it being in the advance disembark
and went out on Guard or Picket.

GEORGE MILLER JOURNAL
Union soldier George Miller, like many serving in both armies, kept a journal of his military experiences. Although this page is undated, it was undoubtedly written shortly after February 6, when the Confederate Fort Henry was surrendered to Union forces.

ing the Civil War. They record a range of topics from complaints about food, shelter and clothing to gossip about past or future battles and the lives of public figures. Official records may provide the actions of military leaders, but the reality of situations was often better revealed in the letters to loved ones.

The correspondence of a Union private and of a Confederate general give insight into what a soldier's life was like in the Civil War. There were many contrasts between Private William Nicholas Fortune of the Union army and

General Mansfield Lovell of the Confederacy. One was a farmer, the other a Northern-born but Southern-inclined aristocrat. One was poor, the other well-to-do. One was a lowly private, the other a general, the commander of thousands. Both men wrote letters to their wives in March 1863, not knowing what the future would bring.

Lovell was waiting for a Court of Inquiry to convene on his decision to evacuate New Orleans, and Private Fortune was awaiting trial by combat at Vicksburg; but both were waiting for something, anything, to happen. The eventual outcome of their waiting ended their involvement in the Civil War.

On March 18, 1863, Will Fortune wrote his wife, Lizzie:

"Lizzie I had hoped that we would stop at this place (Memphis) but our destination is Vicksburg. We are going to stop here long enough to cook up some more provisions to last us down. We will start from here probably tomorrow. It is three hundred and fifty miles (by river) from here to Vicksburg."

By the end of May, Will's cousin, W. H. Fortune, sadly wrote to Lizzie that her beloved husband had died of wounds suffered at Vicksburg. In a letter dated May 30, 1863, he wrote:

"I shall haft to tell you that William has departed from this world & has gone to his . . . home. he has paid the det which all of us owe.

"He was wounded in the charge this last friday week & lived untill this morning . . . They wasant any of us thought he would die he was in good spirits & his wounds doing well but yesterday we could see that they was a great change lizzey. he was taking car of just as well as he could be heare. I think the doctors doen their duty . . . had . . . hopes of him all the time untill yesterday, yesterday he told me that it was a bad change from last night untill this morning he was all together out of his hed. It wasant half of the time that he new me last night."

McCLELLAND SADDLE
Just prior to the Civil War, the recommendations of General George B. McClelland resulted in a new regulation U. S. saddle which was named for him. An adaptation of the high-pommeled Western style, the sturdy and comfortable design had saddle bags and straps for attaching blanket roll or poncho.

In March 1863, at the same time Will Fortune was journeying to Vicksburg, General Mansfield Lovell was in Jackson, Mississippi, waiting to see if the blame for the fall of New Orleans would rest on him. In a letter to his wife, dated March 21, he said:

"The Court of Inquiry has not met yet, are awaiting for Genl Hindman's arrival. The rest are all here, and he is expected daily, as he started some time ago to come to this side of the river (General Hindman was in Arkansas). I saw one of his staff yesterday, just arrived, and he said that the General should be here soon. I do hope he will soon make his appearance here, as it is stupidly dull."

The Court of Inquiry exonerated Mansfield Lovell of all responsibility for the loss of New Orleans, but Jefferson Davis, in a vindictive mood, refused to give him another command. Lovell continued to wait, hoping Davis would change his mind. In July 1864 General Joseph E. Johnston requested that General Lovell be assigned the command of A. P. Stewart's division, but Jefferson Davis ignored the plea. Lovell, realizing that his military career with the Confederacy was over, wrote his wife on July 9, 1864:

" . . . The absurd excuse was given that the President had acted in the matter before he received General Johnston's telegrams about me (Davis had said he had already selected another commander). This, I am well satisfied, was simply a lie, and we are all of the same opinion—I don't know but that, on the whole, I would rather remain as I am, than take command of a division, with no hope of any favors from the people in Richmond. Let them continue their uniform course of malignity and persecution—It will make the record more conclusive in the end."

Lovell was given orders to join Lee's Army of Northern Virginia just two weeks before Lee surrendered to Grant but never had a chance to join his new command.

As the war went on, one of the abiding fears for

FIELD HOSPITAL
Neither army provided adequate medical treatment for the wounded or sick in or out of the field. Wounded were often left on battlefields for days unless they could walk to the nearest forward dressing station. However, more men died from such diseases as septicemia, gangrene, typhoid and pneumonia than from enemy bullets.

soldiers was being wounded as William Fortune had been. The Civil War soldier, whether Union or Confederate, entered military service at a time when the killing power of the weapons used was at peak efficiency. It was also a time when the science of medicine was inadequate to cope with infection and disease. When the soldier fought, he was likely to be seriously wounded; when he encamped, he lived in unsanitary conditions likely to make him sick; and in both cases he rarely received sufficient medical care. Doctors simply knew too little about the causes of disease or infection.

FIELD SURGERY KITS
The brass-bound walnut case at left contains all the medical instruments necessary for an amputation in the field: tourniquet, bone knives, and saw, as well as blunt probes and forceps. At center are delicate instruments for neurological (nerve or brain) surgery backed by the standard medical text of the day: Gray's Anatomy.
A doctor's leather bag is on the right.

The field hospital was a place of horrible agony and suffering. Men brought in with abdominal wounds were left to die because surgeons could do little for them. For arms and legs shattered by the half-inch musket bullets, the only treatment was amputation, usually without any anesthetic, before fatal gangrene could set in. If a surgeon's instruments were rinsed off (they were never sterilized) between operations, the case was an exception. Often the bandages and dressings from infected wounds were simply washed out and used again on new patients. The stench of decaying flesh, the sight of heaps of discarded amputated arms and legs, and the sound of shrieks of pain made the scene of a field hospital a living nightmare.

In military camps diseases such as typhoid, dysentery and pneumonia were rampant. Their causes were unknown and there was no successful treatment for them. Even the childhood disease of measles struck the armies with devastating consequences. The summer of 1861 found one out of every seven Confederates in the Army of Northern Virginia with measles. Few men died from measles alone, but the tendency was to get up too soon, which often led to fatal complications. Confederate Private Alex Jones wrote his wife, Sallie, in Jackson, Tennessee, to let her know that he was leaving the field hospital fully recovered from typhoid fever. He

SURGEON'S MORNING REPORT
Such daily reports by army doctors kept commanders informed of the number of men fit or unfit for duty. This regimental sick list for companies probably in training camp was made a month after the fall of Fort Sumter.

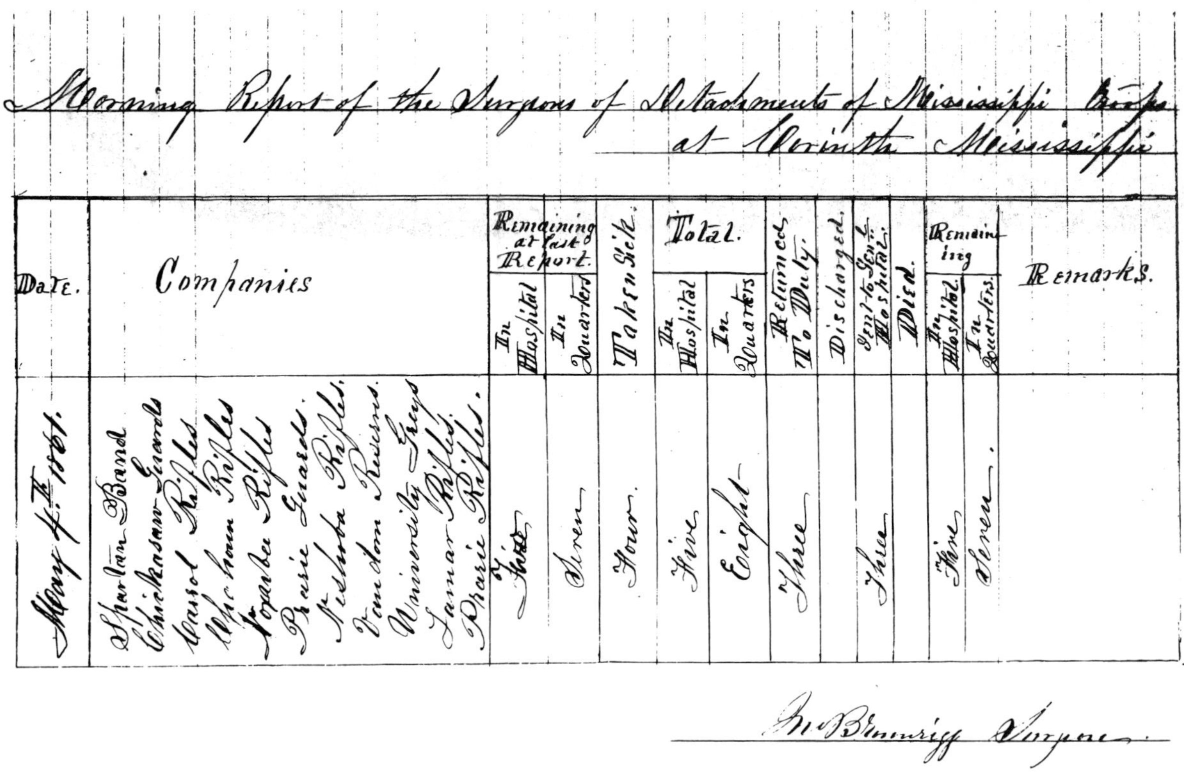

Morning Report of the Surgeon of Detachments of Mississippi Troops at Corinth Mississippi

Date.	Companies	Remaining at last Report: In Hospital	Remaining at last Report: In Quarters	Taken Sick.	Total: In Hospital	Total: In Quarters	Returned to Duty.	Discharged.	Sent to Genl. Hospital.	Died.	Remaining: In Hospital	Remaining: In Quarters	Remarks.
May 4th 1861.	[illegible] Band, Chickasaw Guards, [illegible] Rifles, Calhoun Rifles, Noxubee Rifles, Prairie Guards, Neshoba Rifles, Van Dorn Reserves, University Greys, Lamar Rifles, Prairie Rifles.	Five	Seven	Four	Five	Eight	Three		Three		Five	Seven.	

[illegible] Surgeon.

was one of the lucky ones, because more soldiers died from disease than in battle. On the Confederate side the ratio was three to one (the total Confederate dead numbered 258,000), while for every Union combat casualty, two soldiers died from disease (the total Union dead was 359,000).

Those, like Alex Jones, who were fortunate enough to recover and be returned fit for duty, began to find the tempo of life changing. The war was speeding up, and the times of leisurely reading and writing letters, playing cards, reading the Bible, repairing clothes and recording experiences in a diary or journal were fewer and and fewer. Camp life was still boring, but the struggle to survive was beginning to make those long days between battles earlier in the war seem like a holiday from death.

Food was scarce, and soldiers had to forage far afield or keep moving to areas as yet untouched by the war. Such was the case for Private Hubbard and the men of the 7th Cavalry in July 1864 when they came to the "rich prairie country below Okolona, Mississippi." Even years later he could recall the fields full of watermelons, roasting ears of corn and fat hogs. The hungry troops had "plenty of greasy bacon and some with a streak of lean and a streak of fat," which was held on a sharpened stick over a fire and gobbled down as soon as it had begun to sizzle and curl in the smoke. Those who still had some captured coffee and sugar finished off their meal with a steaming cup while others had to make do with a "chaw," dip or smoke of tobacco.

Winter was the worst season in a soldier's life. As the war neared a conclusion, winter was a time of discomfort, privation and boredom, because the days were not even broken up by the loathed task of drilling. The only thing a soldier could do in the field was to spend all the time and effort he could to make his quarters as comfortable as possible.

A squad would combine its resources and build huts of wood from fences or saplings cut from a nearby grove

LETTER WRITING EQUIPMENT
Letters written with a steel-pointed pen and thick ink by anxious wives, mothers, sisters and sweethearts were weighed on postage scales before being mailed or were slipped through the lines to their loved ones in the army.

and increase their size by digging out the interior. Nails were driven into walls to provide hooks for hanging clothes and equipment. Bayonets were stuck into the floors or walls to provide stands for candles so the soldiers could pass the time reading or playing cards. Some, like the lucky troopers of Company E, 7th Tennessee Cavalry, CSA, were comfortably "quartered" in the vacant storehouses at Coldwater, Mississippi, 31 miles from Memphis, "when the snow began to fly."

WINTER QUARTERS
Although commissioned and non-commissioned officers took over the more comfortable abandoned buildings, veteran soldiers learned to prepare warm shelters for winter with whatever materials or buildings were available.

INFANTRYMAN
With all his possessions in a blanket roll tied at each end and slung across his shoulders, a Confederate foot soldier could travel faster and farther than his Union counterpart, who carried a cumbersome and heavy field pack.

"The men provided themselves with heavier clothing," recalled Private John Milton Hubbard, "some articles of which were brought through the lines from home, while others were secured through blockade runners, as those citizens were called who carried cotton to Memphis and brought out supplies on a Federal permit. The service was light, with no picket duty, for the winter was so cold and the roads so bad that a Federal raid could hardly be expected. But the hours could be whiled away. So, when the boys were not rubbing up their arms and grooming their horses, they were cutting firewood, playing poker or dancing. . . . Boots were heavy, but the dancers were muscular and strong. They could thread the Virginia reel or tread through the mazes of a quartet, but the eight-couple cotillion, in which a greater number could participate (gave) more spirit to the amusement. . . . "

Whether it was singing or dancing or listening, both armies found music a great morale builder and outlet for soldiers longing for home and family. Soldiers of both sides preferred sentimental ballads to military marches. "The Girl I Left Behind Me" had a spirited tempo that could brighten marching feet, but in the evening the nostalgically sad "Tenting Tonight on the Old Camp Ground" would make eyes grow moist as they stared into the campfire.

Ironically, the songs which the armies made their own were borrowed from each other. "Dixie" was a Northern minstrel song, written by Dan Emmett, the son of an abolitionist, and the music for Julia Ward Howe's "The Battle Hymn of the Republic" was sung as a Southern campmeeting hymn in the late 1850's.

Military music also had its place in the soldier's life. Many of the Union and Confederate regiments started the war with complete bands, but when active campaigning began, the bands became a luxury and were soon replaced by the fife and drum corps. Fife and drum units remained with both sides throughout the war and sounded all the military commands. Members of these units were under the surgeon's command, and it was their duty during a battle to care for the wounded on the battlefield. Over 40,000 musicians served in the Union army and almost as many in the Confederate army. Letters to people back home often spoke of the inspiration received by the men at the front from the

CARD GAME
Games of all kinds provided a means of passing the long, dreary hours in camp.

shrill fifes and booming drums formed up with the battle line.

But nothing took the place of letters from home. These were saved and treasured, read and reread at every opportunity, and bits of news shared with friends. Alex Jones, the trooper in Forrest's Cavalry, managed to send and receive letters by friends going home on furlough or sneaking through the Federal lines around Jackson, Tennessee. The letter written by his wife, Sallie, on May 22, 1864, expressing her yearning and concern for him, also hinted of the war weariness affecting the entire South.

"Dear husband I have just received your letter this morning which was a sorce of pleasure to me. I seat myself this lovely sabbath day to wright you a few lines. This leaves all well hoping and ever wishing they will reach you enjoying the blessings. Mr. Jones I have nothing new to wright, we are getting along with our crop tolerable well. I had to plant the first piece of cotton over as far as I could get seed. where the good seed was planted there is a very good stand. Mr. Jones we have been hearing great news that the south was so victorious I began to think the war would soon be over but the northern papers of a later date gives a different account of the fight in Virginia. . . . Mr. Jones it is thought that forrest will go to georgia. I want to ask you one more time for my sake not to go. Mr. Jones if I was in your place I would come home if forrest went to georgia or to Virginia either place I would risk the consequences at any rate. I must close we are looking for Mr. Moore and his wife. They will stay with us to night. I would be glad you was here with me and the children to day. They are the two sweetest little cubs in the world I think. Mr. Jones wright soon, you have my prayers ever. May the lord keep you in my prayers as I wright."

Sallie would have to wait another 12 months and 13 days for her Alex to come home to her and the "two sweetest cubs in the world." But Lizzie Fortune would never see her Will again, nor Mariam Forrest Luxton her sons Jeffrey and Aaron. For them and others like them, there would be no homecoming.

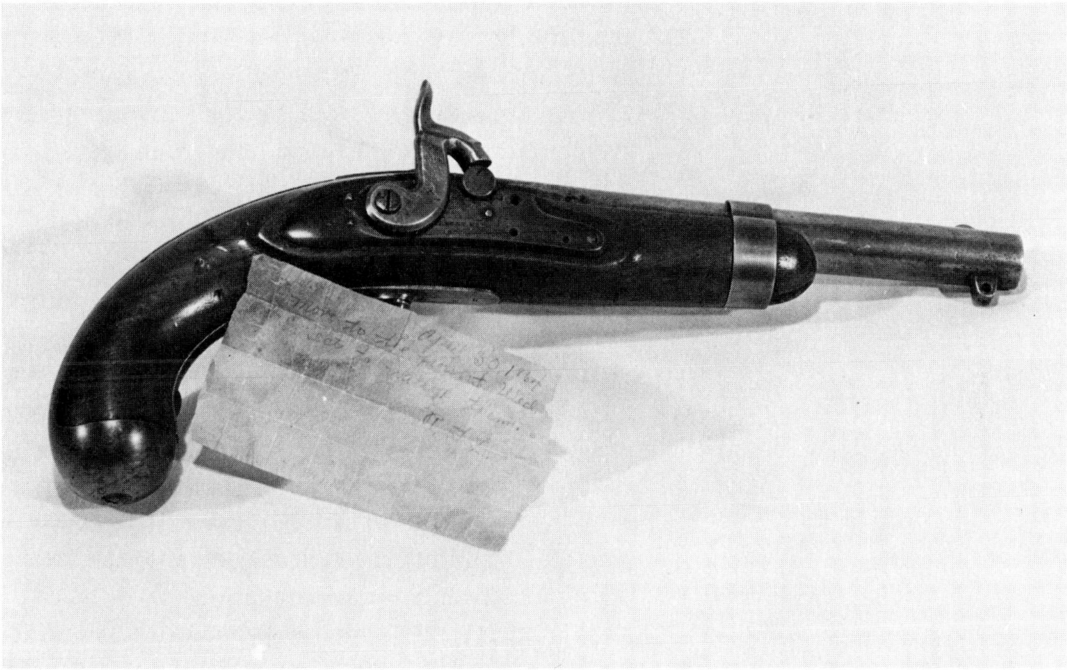

CONVERTED FLINTLOCK PISTOL
This 1837 single-shot flintlock pistol made by the historic arms manufacturing firm of Asa Holman Waters in Millbury, Massachusetts, was converted to percussion cap use and carried during the Civil War by a Memphian's ancestor. When disassembling the gun for cleaning, a Pink Palace Museum staff member discovered a penciled message on brown oiled paper concealed in the butt. Dated April 30, 1864, the note read: "Move to the front Wed. Expect to wallop them. R. G. L."

CHAPTER 3

Nightmare on the Glory Road

U.S. UNIFORM
Representative of the types of uniforms worn by Union soldiers.

OLD MEN cheered and mothers and sweethearts wept as the flower of Southern youth marched confidently from Memphis to join the thin line of 48,000 Confederate troops defending the 600-mile northern border of Tennessee. The fortifications on this line were completely inadequate and were, for the most part, poorly manned with ill-equipped, raw recruits.

Just as a multitheater strategy evolved in World War II because of geographic boundaries, so did this need become evident early in the Civil War. When Jefferson Davis moved the capital of the Confederacy from Montgomery, Alabama, to Richmond, Virginia, in 1861, the Union goal in the East became the capture of Richmond, and all offensive military strategy revolved around this aim.

The Union plan in the West hinged on capturing control of the three rivers which were the avenues that led to the heart of the South: the Mississippi, the Tennessee and the Cumberland Rivers. In addition to the line of fortifications along the Mississippi River, there were twin forts just south of the Kentucky state line: Fort Henry on the Tennessee River and Fort Donelson on the Cumberland River. If these could be breached by the Federal army, their fall would open Middle Tennessee, including Nashville, to invasion. This loss would compel the Confederates to withdraw their forces from Bowling Green, Kentucky, causing the Southern armies in the West to move their defensive lines to northern Alabama and Mississippi.

This plan was set in motion in early February 1862 when Union General Ulysses S. Grant left Cairo, Illinois, with 15,000 men and a small fleet of river gunboats commanded by Commodore Andrew Foote and steamed toward the weakest link in the chain – Fort Henry.

Located on the east bank of the Tennessee River, which was subject to extraordinary rises of water, Fort Henry was a "paper fort." On paper it seemed powerful, but in reality the fort had been sited in lowlands that were subject to flooding. At the beginning of February as the winter snows began to melt, the Tennessee River was high and much of Fort Henry was already inundated. To correct this defensive oversight, the Confederates had hastily tried to construct another fort, named Heiman, on a higher site on the west bank. This new fort was still not finished, and, as the Federal force approached, the garrison of 1,100 Confederates was hurriedly evacuated to Fort Henry.

Before the major battle began on February 6, 1862, the rapidly rising Tennessee River overflowed into the lower main powder magazine, and the Rebel commander, realizing Fort Henry was indefensible, sent most of his men cross-country to Fort Donelson, keeping only enough to work the cannon bearing on the river.

The battle had not lasted long, but the blasted walls and demolished guns of Fort Henry were evidence of its ferocity. Over 400 screaming shells had been poured into the citadel by Foote's river fleet. The Rebel gunners, in spite of their accurate placement of 59 hits on the gunboats, had no shells large enough to sink or even cripple the Union fleet. The best they could manage was to disable one gunboat.

Confederate Brigadier General Floyd Tilghman left Fort Donelson to take personal charge of Fort Henry's defense, but, by the time he arrived, the heavy guns had been silenced and Grant's Union infantry was encircling the fort, ready to slam the back door shut. Because the fort could not be saved, Tilghman sent the supporting infantry to Fort Donelson and ordered Fort Henry

CSA ARTILLERYMAN
Confederate uniforms varied from ragged to resplendent. This artilleryman wears kepi (cap), sash and high boots with spurs.

HORNET'S NEST
Union Generals W. H. L. Wallace and B. M. Prentiss rallied 1,000 men in a sunken road on the first day of Shiloh. Their unit fought stubbornly for eight hours until Wallace was mortally wounded and Prentiss was captured with a handful of survivors.

to surrender. The defenders from Fort Donelson looked with dismay at the haggard faces of Henry's survivors and realized their turn was next.

With the capture of Fort Henry, Grant focused his attention on Fort Donelson. He sent Foote's fleet up the Tennessee River, across the Ohio River and then down the Cumberland River, while he marched his army overland. But Grant's easy victory over Fort Henry would not be repeated at Fort Donelson since this fort was well-sited and constructed in addition to being heavily armed. It was manned by 20,000 Confederates, among whom were Lieutenant Colonel Nathan Bedford Forrest and his command, under Brigadier Generals John B. Floyd, Simon Bolivar Buckner and Gideon J. Pillow. Grant's plan of attack called for surrounding the Confederates on land while the Union gunboats assaulted the river fortifications. Foote's boats would then pound the defenses to a point where a successful infantry assault could capture the fort.

The plan might have worked to perfection had Foote not brought his gunboats within range of the fort's guns. This mistake was costly for the Federals since the Confederates repeatedly slammed shots into the gunboats, causing terrible carnage. Numbers of men were killed and others horribly mangled. In a short time the squadron withdrew with two severely mauled boats and several others damaged. Foote himself had been badly wounded. The next day, February 15, the Confederates raised their rebel yell and raced for the right of the Union line. Several Union brigades broke and ran headlong in retreat, swinging open the door of escape for the encircled garrison. But Grant realized the Confederates had weakened their right in order to mount the attack, and he sent a counterattack, which caused the Confederates to withdraw disappointed and exhausted into the fort. That night, Grant was heavily reinforced, bringing his command to 40,000 men. He was confident the next day would bring the fall of Fort Donelson.

On the evening of February 15 an officers' council was called in the fort. The situation seemed very grave to the commanding generals because one of the flanks of the fort had been compromised and the Confederates were outnumbered two to one. The three brigadier generals had no clear-cut command authority and debated the situation late into the night. Even though both General Pillow and General Floyd wanted to fight their way through the Union lines, hoping to save the remaining 18,000-man force, the persuasive Buckner convinced them that to do so would mean the loss of thousands. It was finally decided that the fort would be surrendered by Buckner.

According to Civil War historian Bruce Catton, Buckner was chosen because he was a long-time army friend of Grant's and there was a greater chance he would escape any possible vengeance of the Lincoln government. No Confederate generals had yet been captured, and it was not known if they would be treated as prisoners of war or tried as treasonous citizens. Floyd, as the former Secretary of War in President Buchanan's

PRESTON SMITH UNIFORM
Preston Smith, a Memphis lawyer at the beginning of the war, received a commission as colonel of the 154th Senior Tennessee Infantry Regiment. He was severely wounded at Shiloh but recovered to serve as a member of Polk's Corps at Chickamauga, where he was killed. He is one of several Confederate generals buried in Memphis' Elmwood Cemetery.

Cabinet, stood in special jeopardy because the North believed he had used his official position to supply Southern arsenals and forts with war materials. So the decision was made to pass the command to Buckner and for Pillow and Floyd to leave as soon as possible.

Lieutenant Colonel Forrest took 700 men out of the fort that night along a marshy route between Union forces, and Generals Floyd and Pillow with 5,000 men also escaped successfully and moved toward Clarksville, Tennessee. The next morning the Confederate flag was lowered and the Stars and Stripes fluttered over the fort in its place. The Confederates had 1,200 casualties and lost over 13,000 men as prisoners, including General Buckner. Adding insult to injury, two regiments of Confederates, unaware of the fort's surrender and intended as reinforcements, marched into the fort on February 17 and were added to the list of prisoners. Also lost were 3,000 horses, 48 field guns, 17 pieces of heavy artillery, 20,000 muskets and an immense quantity of supplies—a heavy blow to an underequipped Confederacy.

General Floyd was relieved of all further command by Jefferson Davis, even though no court of inquiry was convened. General Pillow was absolved by the Confederate high command, but Jefferson Davis would not give him another meaningful command during the war. Pillow was finally assigned to the volunteer and conscript bureau in Tennessee and became a commissary general of prisoners in February 1865. Buckner, who was exchanged as a prisoner of war, returned to the Confederacy to serve in many important commands, despite his insistence on the surrender of Fort Donelson.

The loss of Fort Donelson made the front pages of the Memphis papers and caused a severe drop in Confederate morale since the whole state of Tennessee was now open to invasion by Union forces and the defense of Alabama and Mississippi was threatened. This, perhaps more than Shiloh or Vicksburg, was the turning point of the war in the West. The Memphis papers also anxiously followed General Grant's advance through

Tennessee, an advance which forced Confederate General Albert Sidney Johnston to fall back from Bowling Green, Kentucky, to Corinth, Mississippi. By early April the Union forces were poised near the Mississippi border, just north of the South's only east-west rail link, the Memphis & Charleston Railroad. To counteract General Grant's advance, General Johnston assembled an army of 45,000 Confederates at Shiloh.

On April 6, 1862, Grant's troops were awakened by rebel yells and volleys of musket fire. Johnston hit Grant at Pickwick Landing, Tennessee, near Shiloh Church, in a surprise attack that sent the Union army reeling. Whole Union regiments disintegrated before the hard-charging Confederates. Union Generals Benjamin Prentiss and W. H. L. Wallace gathered about 2,000 men around them and slowed the Confederate advance by their courageous stand in the "Hornet's Nest." This sunken road was so named because the Union troops there were subjected to the sting of thousands of Confederate musket shots and deafening bombardment from massed cannon. As the Union troops began to crumble under the savage Rebel fire, they saw the determined General Wallace fall mortally wounded, and they eventually surrendered. But their valor had bought Grant the time he needed to reorganize his fleeing army and to make a stand with massed artillery at Pickwick

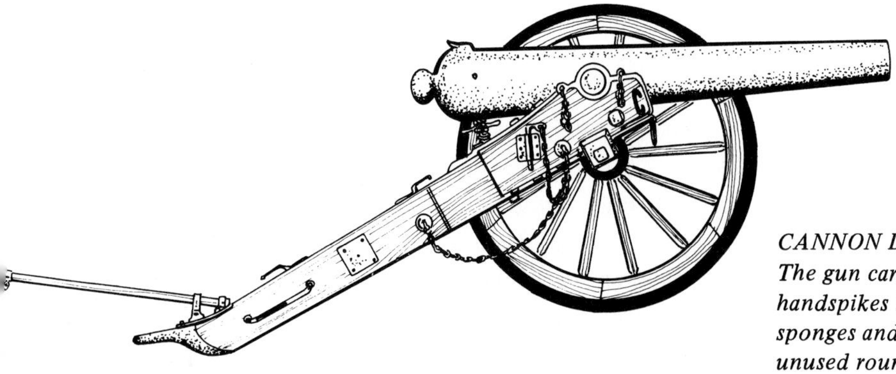

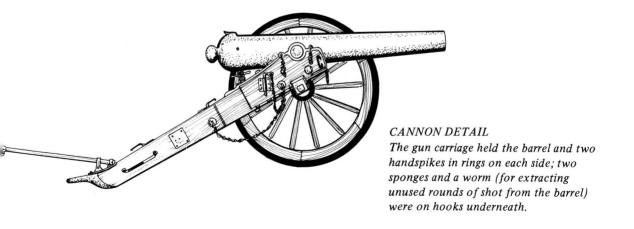

CANNON DETAIL
The gun carriage held the barrel and two handspikes in rings on each side; two sponges and a worm (for extracting unused rounds of shot from the barrel) were on hooks underneath.

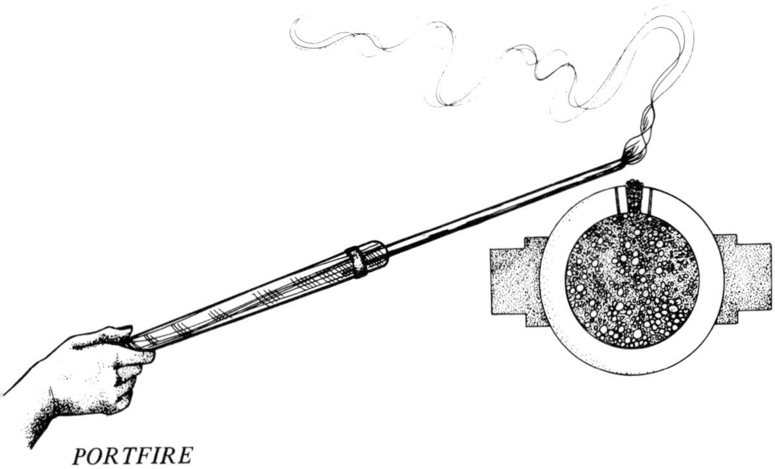

PORTFIRE
Portfire was a combustible substance wrapped in a paper tube which, once lighted, burned so intensely it could not be extinguished even by rain. The cannon's venthole was filled with gunpowder which ignited when touched by the portfire's flame. This method of cannon detonation was soon abandoned because of accidents from premature firing.

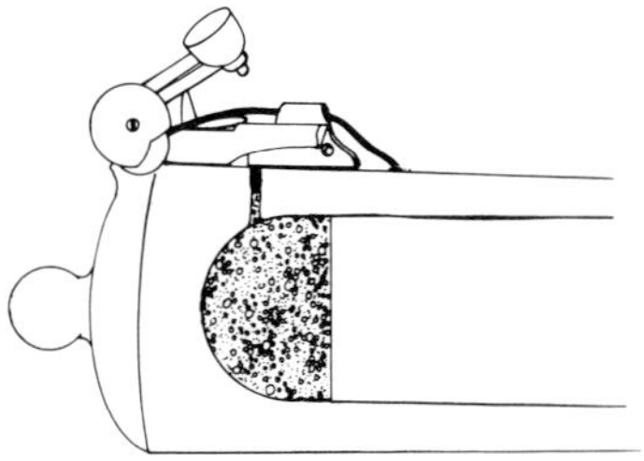

HAMMER
The hammer was used with a quill priming tube, a major step forward in firing devices, which did away with the necessity for priming with loose powder from a flask or horn. The tube was ignited by the hammer of a lock striking an explosive wafer laid on top of the cup prior to firing.

Landing. Grant was also aided by Union gunboats bombarding the Confederate right wing.

As night came on, the two armies took stock of their losses. The Federals had lost General Prentiss and 2,000 men as prisoners; they also lost General Wallace, who died of wounds sustained in the "Hornet's Nest." The Confederates had lost their commanding general, Albert Sidney Johnston. The General had been critically wounded in a leg artery and bled to death before he could receive medical attention. Both armies lay exhausted on a field cluttered with the debris of battle and the already mangled bodies of fallen comrades and enemies. The hard rain which fell that night provided refreshment to those recovering from the fever of battle, but not to those lying wounded in the fresh mud.

Grant's army was saved by the arrival during the night of reinforcements commanded by General Lew Wallace (author of *Ben Hur*) and General Don Carlos Buell. The next morning, April 7, Grant determined to launch an all-out counterattack. He believed the Confederates could be easily swept before his refreshed and reinforced troops, but he had not counted on the Con-

FRICTION PRIMER
The friction primer became the most popular device for firing muzzle-loading cannon during the Civil War. It had a self-contained powder charge in a tube which was inserted into the vent. When the lanyard attached to the loop of serrated wire within the tube was pulled, it created a spark, much like striking a match on a rough surface, and ignited the powder charge.

federates' stubborn resistance. Although the two armies battled for hours the next day, the Union army made little progress. Finally, worn down by two days of hard fighting, the Confederate defense collapsed, and the soldiers began to fall back rapidly, leaving the field to the Northerners. Grant's cavalry under General William T. Sherman was so exhausted it made only a half-hearted attempt to pursue the Rebels as they retreated 18 miles south to Corinth, Mississippi.

As the initial reports of Shiloh came into Memphis and the newspapers recounted the first day of battle, Memphians believed it to be a great Southern victory. Their hopes were dashed, however, as later news revealed the Confederate army was in full retreat. Anxious relatives of men fighting at Shiloh fearfully studied the casualty lists posted in the city. The number of losses was appalling: the Union loss in dead, wounded or missing was 13,047; Confederate casualties numbered 10,694.

Skirmishing continued around Corinth for the next month, until the eight-day siege of Corinth began in earnest on May 21. After sustaining heavy losses on

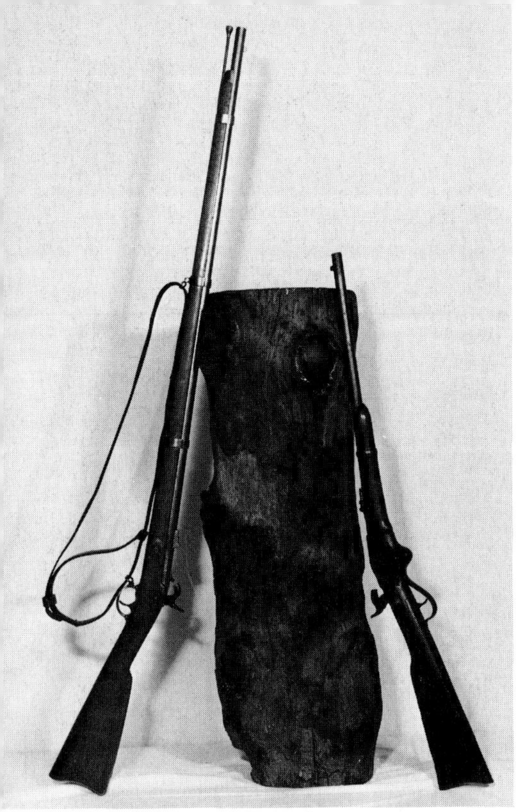

MUSKET AND CARBINE
A remnant of the past and a forecast of the future came together at Shiloh. Leaning against a tree stump from Shiloh is a long-barreled smoothbore, muzzle-loading musket (at left), which was made obsolete by the close of the Civil War because of improved weapon technology. An example of this technology is the breech-loaded, rapid-firing carbine rifle at right, a forerunner of modern automatic weapons.

May 29, the routed Confederates destroyed what they could not carry away, and for five miles along the withdrawal route the roads were littered with arms, equipment and supplies discarded by the exhausted troops.

One last attempt would be made by the Confederates to retake Corinth. On the morning of October 4, 1862, Confederate forces numbering 38,000 men under Generals Earl Van Dorn, Sterling "Pap" Price and Mansfield Lovell attacked the Union breastworks (temporary fortifications made of earth) surrounding Corinth and defended by 20,000 men under General W. S. Rosecrans. The Union forces were driven back into town, but the Confederates could not breach the inner fortifications because of their heavy losses. When the battle resumed the next day, the Confederates were forced to retreat.

The defeat of Confederate forces at Shiloh in April 1862 and the Confederate withdrawal from Corinth in May left the eastern door to Memphis wide open and unprotected. The city had not fortified its riverfront because it believed the forts upriver and downriver offered adequate protection. Memphians also saw little need for building defenses on the eastern approaches because of the protection afforded by Forts Henry and Donelson.

Memphians knew the importance of the Mississippi River as the transportation link that bound the Confederate West together. They realized the absence of several thousand able-bodied men in the Confederate Army left the city poorly equipped to resist Union land and naval forces. After the Confederate retreat at Corinth, Memphis had neither the time nor the manpower to erect fortifications. While Corinth was being taken by Union forces in northern Mississippi, Tennessee Forts Pillow and Randolph, upriver from Memphis on the first and second Chickasaw Bluffs, were evacuated because they were no longer defensible.

The compromise of Memphis' defense took place not only along the Tennessee and Cumberland Rivers but also along the Mississippi River. While General

BREASTWORKS AT CORINTH
The evacuation of Corinth in May 1862 left the back door of Memphis open for Grant's army. The battle of Corinth, fought between October 3 and 5, 1862, brought northern Mississippi under Union control.

Grant was preparing to attack Fort Henry on the Tennessee River, Union General John Pope began his campaign against the Mississippi River forts. In early 1862, Pope's Union gunboats engaged the defenders of Columbus, Kentucky, in a fierce artillery duel. The heavy fire of the gunboats outslugged that of the fort, and after several days of fighting, the Confederates abandoned Columbus. When the Union troops entered on March 3, they saw nothing but destruction. Empty boxes, scattered tins, demolished guns, burned and gutted quarters all attested to the rapid departure of the Confederates.

With his 12,000-man army and several gunboats, Union General Pope now turned his attention to New Madrid, Missouri, and the fortifications on Island Number 10. The attack began in the middle of March when Union gunboats lobbed hundreds of shells into the fortifications of Island Number 10. In spite of heavy bombardment, the Confederate defenders tenaciously and courageously held on to their position. The turning

U.S. INFANTRYMAN
The Union infantryman was usually well-equipped. Any shortages were temporary and due to an overburdened Quartermaster Corps.

ELLET RAM (Side View)
This model of the Ellet ram by William G. Ballenger of Chicago is featured in the Mississippi River Museum/Mud Island as part of the Introduction to the Civil War exhibit. The scale is ¼ inch to 1 foot; the model measures 20¾ inches × 47 inches × 15½ inches.

ELLET RAM (Front View)
Charles Ellet, Jr. specially designed these boats to operate on inland waterways. He strengthened the hulls of river steamers and filled the bows with solid timbers, enclosing the boilers in a double tier of 24-inch-thick oak. Only the pilothouse was armored, so crews were reluctant to serve on them until they proved their worth in the Battle of Memphis. Courtesy of Mississippi River Museum/Mud Island *(Memphis, Tennessee)*

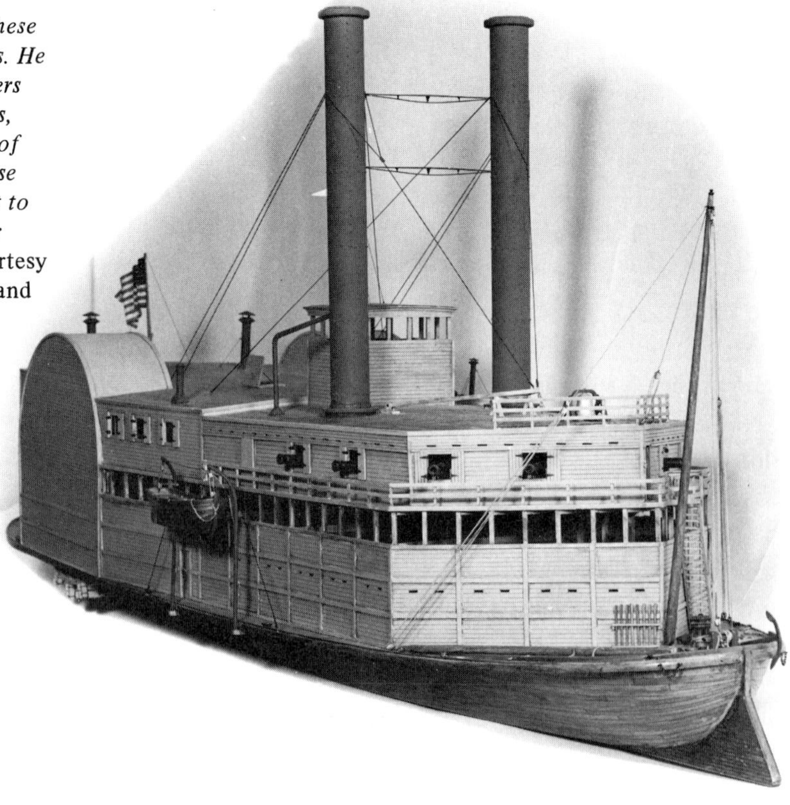

point in the campaign came when Colonel Roberts led 50 volunteers from the 42nd Illinois Regiment, along with 50 sailors, in a lightning raid on the island's upper fort. In a matter of minutes these gallant men scampered up the fortification's embankments, beating back the gun crews, and disabled the fort's cannon. Then they slipped back to the safety of their boats. Loss of this fire power severely handicapped the island's defenses and allowed several Union divisions to land there on April 7. On this same day, Grant's army was routing the Confederates at Shiloh.

The main Confederate force in the area of Island Number 10 was encamped near the present site of Tiptonville, Tennessee. With the fall of the fort this army of 6,000, including four generals, 2,000 horses and mules, 1,000 supply wagons holding $40,000 worth of supplies, and 10,000 muskets began a hasty retreat. Before they had gone far, they were overtaken on the flat, open floodplain by the fast-moving Union army of 12,000 men. The loss of Island Number 10 and its supporting force caused the Confederates to evacuate Forts Randolph and Pillow.

The Rebel troops that left these forts on June 4 were sent to guard the north-south route of the Mobile and Ohio Railway in northern Mississippi. The river road to Memphis was now open.

When New Orleans fell to Commodore David G. Farragut's gunboats and General Benjamin F. Butler's Union army took control on April 29, Memphis, Tennessee, and Vicksburg, Mississippi, became the Confederacy's last two major strategic points on the Mississippi River. The South's military leaders made the decision to evacuate Memphis and fortify Vicksburg, which could be more easily defended because of its natural barriers to invasion. The only frail defense Memphis could muster against the overwhelming troops of Grant and the Union river fleet was a squadron of gunboat-rams stationed at the waterfront.

This flotilla, called the River Defense Fleet, was under the command of J. E. (Ed) Montgomery (pilot-

BENJAMIN FRANKLIN CHEATHAM
General Cheatham was the brigade commander at Belmont, Missouri, and a division commander at Shiloh. He fought with distinction in every engagement of the Army of Tennessee.

teacher of Mark Twain) and consisted of eight remodeled steamboats. The machinery and boilers propelling the boats were protected by an inner and an outer bulkhead of heavy timber, with bales of cotton compressed to fit into the 22-inch space between the bulkheads. This whole bulkhead, or wall, was covered with railroad iron an inch thick, and the bows were filled with heavy timber with iron strips bent around the prow at the front of the boat to make ramming more effective. Each boat carried one 24-pounder and two 32-pounder cannon and some of the rams had an additional 8-inch rifled cannon. All this armament was light by naval standards and no match for the much heavier firepower of the Union gunboats. These ironclads, which were nicknamed "cotton-clads," had been in service only two months by June 1862 but had already covered themselves with glory in a skirmish with Union gunboats several miles upriver from Memphis at Plum Point Bend.

Montgomery's flagship was called the *Little Rebel* and was a former seagoing ship with a screw propeller. Five of the eight cotton-clads had been named for popular Confederate generals: *Beauregard*, *Bragg*, *Price*, *Jeff Thompson* and *Van Dorn*. The two remaining boats were named the *Sumter* and the *Colonel Lovell* (sometimes confused with another boat called the *General Lovell*).

Memphis had a naval shipyard, and in early 1862 two giant steam rams, the *Arkansas* and the *Tennessee*, were under construction there. Shortly before the battle of Memphis, the *Arkansas* had been launched but not outfitted for service, so it was towed downriver to safety. The *Tennessee*, however, was still on its stocks in the waterfront yard and had to be destroyed by the retreating Confederates to prevent its use by the Union forces.

In the settling darkness of June 5, 1862, the Federal gunboats anchored at the bend of the river just above Memphis. Spreading themselves out in a line of battle across the river with the rams, other supply and troop boats upstream of them, they waited for dawn and battle.

After long deliberation and much disagreement, the Confederates decided to attack the Union boats the next morning, even though the swift current of the flood-swollen Mississippi was against them, giving the Union boats an advantage. General Jeff Thompson, who resented Montgomery's command and his battle plan, left the cotton-clads with his sharpshooting Missouri troops. The morning would prove that their absence made little difference to the outcome.

There were mixed emotions among Memphians that night as they awaited the battle. Many expected to cheer a Southern naval victory; the more pragmatic began taking precautionary measures. Cotton that had been stored in riverfront warehouses, awaiting shipment to the coast and then to England, was burned so that it would not be used by the Union army. The management of the *Memphis Daily Appeal* loaded its newspaper press and staff on a train for Grenada, Mississippi.

As day was breaking on that fateful June 6, the ever broadening rays of the rising sun fell upon a crowd of 10,000 anxious Memphians lining the bluff that overlooked the river. What feelings of pride mixed with trepidation must have filled their hearts as they saw the little Confederate squadron steam out into the flood-driven current to meet its destiny.

The massed citizenry looked on as the Union gunboats came downriver in a single line of battle with their sterns pointed downstream. This position was necessary because of the difficulty involved in backing in the swift-flowing river in case of damage or the need for maneuvering. The Union gunboats were led by Commodore C. H. Davis, with Colonel Charles Ellet Jr. commanding the rams he had specially designed for the Mississippi River.

At 5:30 A.M. the Confederates opened fire with their light cannon, and the Union gunboats, still out of their range, responded, but without damage to either side. Within a matter of minutes, however, the Union

MAYOR JOHN PARK
After the defeat of the Confederate gunboats in the Battle of Memphis, Mayor John Park was forced to surrender the defenseless city to the Union forces.

rams, propelled like torpedoes by the surging current, entered the fight. The *Queen of the West*, commanded by Ellet, and the *Monarch*, commanded by his brother, were the first to engage the cotton-clads. The *Queen* bore headlong for the *Lovell*, which had just lost its commander to a Union sharpshooter. The *Lovell* turned broadside while trying to maneuver out of the way but was rammed by the *Queen*. The collision was so great that the *Lovell* was cut in half and sank so rapidly many men drowned in the swift current or were trapped in the ship's wreckage. Before the *Queen* could free herself from the *Lovell*, she was in turn rammed by the *Beauregard*. A Confederate sharpshooter on the *Beauregard* got a quick glimpse of Colonel Ellet and shot him in the knee. Ellet, lying in an ever-enlarging pool of

his own blood, continued to give orders and eventually brought the disabled *Queen* to the Arkansas shore.

The Rebel *Beauregard* was joined by the *Price,* and together they tried to ram the Union's *Monarch*; but the *Beauregard* missed the quickly maneuvered Federal boat and rammed the Confederate *Price* instead, tearing off its paddle wheel and putting it out of action. The *Beauregard* tried once again to ram the *Monarch* but was outmaneuvered. Turning swiftly with the current at its back, the *Monarch* struck the *Beauregard* on the bow, tearing a gaping hole beneath its waterline. Because the

BATTLE OF MEMPHIS

This Harper's Weekly *sketch of the naval battle before Memphis on June 6, 1862, shows the Federal ram* Monarch *running down the Confederate cottonclad* Beauregard *in the center. In the background is the steep Memphis bluff where the apprehensive citizens watched as their fate was sealed by the destruction of the Confederate flotilla.*

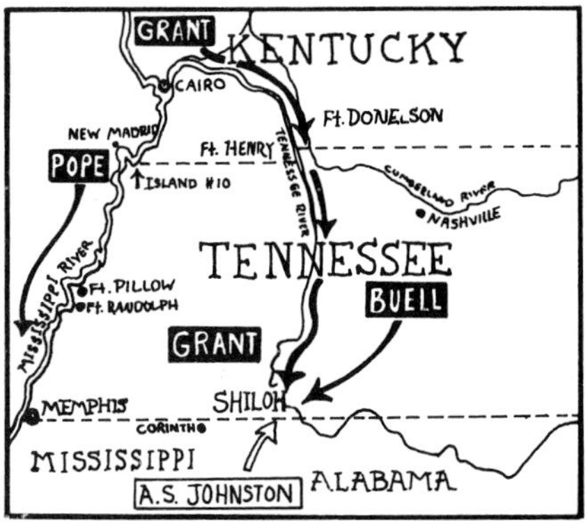

WESTERN THEATER MAP

MAJOR BATTLES OF THE CIVIL WAR IN THE WEST

1861

April 12-14	Attack on Fort Sumter, Charleston, S.C.—Civil War begins in the East
July 5	Engagement at Carthage, Missouri
August 10	Engagement at Wilson's Creek, Missouri
September 2	Capture of Fort Scott, Missouri
November 7	Battle of Belmont, Missouri

1862

January 19-20	Battle of Mill Springs, Missouri
February 6	Capture of Fort Henry, Tennessee
February 16	Capture of Fort Donelson, Tennessee
March 5-8	Battle of Pea Ridge, Arkansas
April 6-7	Battle of Shiloh, Tennessee
April 7	Capture of Island Number 10
April 28	Capture of New Orleans, Louisiana
May 30	Capture of Corinth, Mississippi
June 5	Capture of Fort Pillow, Tennessee
June 6	Battle of Memphis, Tennessee
September 14-16	Battle of Munfordsville, Kentucky
September 19	Battle of Iuka, Mississippi
October 3-4	Battle of Corinth, Mississippi
October 8	Battle of Perryville, Kentucky
December 29	Sherman's repulse at Vicksburg, Mississippi

1863

December 31-January 2	Battle of Murfreesboro, Tennessee
May 16	Fighting at Champion Hill, Mississippi
July 4	Capture of Vicksburg, Mississippi
July 9	Capture of Port Hudson, Louisiana
September 9	Occupation of Chattanooga, Tennessee
September 19-20	Battle of Chickamauga, Georgia
November 23-25	Battle of Chattanooga, Tennessee
December 6	Occupation of Knoxville, Tennessee

1864

February 14	Occupation of Meridian, Mississippi
April 8	Battle of Sabine Cross Roads, Louisiana
May 13-16	Fighting at Resaca, Georgia
May 18	Fighting at Rome, Georgia
June 27	Battle of Kenesaw Mountain, Georgia
July 22	First battle before Atlanta, Georgia
August 5	Capture of Mobile Bay, Alabama
September 2	Capture of Atlanta, Georgia
September 26-27	Fighting at Ironton, Missouri
November 30	Battle of Franklin, Tennessee
December 15-16	Battle of Nashville, Tennessee
December 20	Capture of Savannah, Georgia

1865

May 26	Kirby Smith's surrender at Baton Rouge, Louisiana

Beauregard was doomed and had begun to sink, her crew surrendered. The *Monarch* then pursued Montgomery's flagship, the *Little Rebel*, which, in a race for the safety of the Arkansas shore, ran aground in shallow water and was abandoned by her crew.

As Montgomery and his men waded ashore, they could look out over the scene of battle. They saw the hope of victory die as the badly confused and disorganized Confederate vessels fell prey, one by one, to the accurate fire of the Union gunboats. The remaining four Confederate cotton-clads headed for the Arkansas shore, hoping that their crews could escape. The *Jeff*

SURRENDER OF MEMPHIS
These two brief notes between C. H. Davis, Flag Officer of the Steamer "Benton," and John Park, Mayor of Memphis, brought an end to Confederate Memphis.

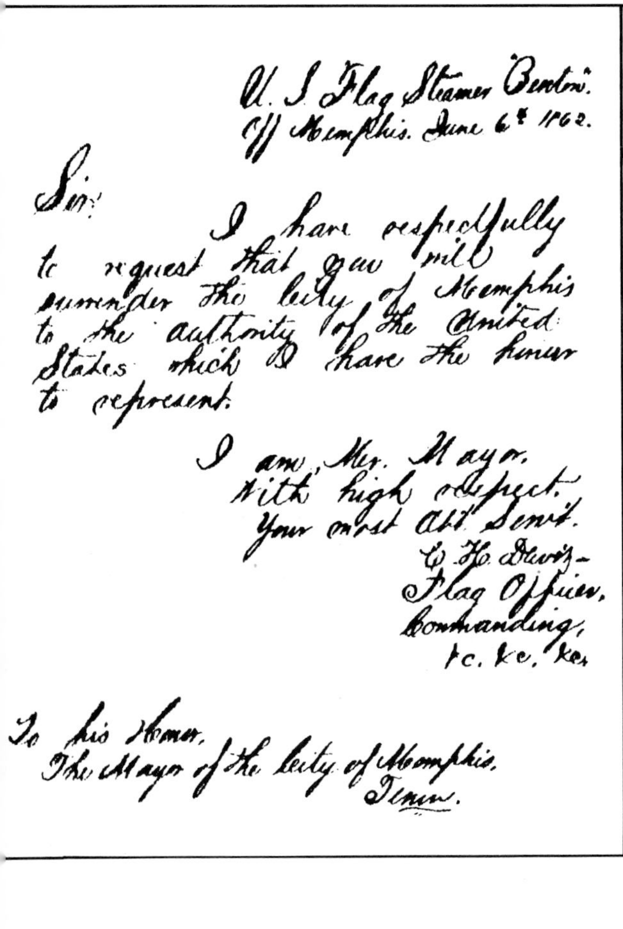
U. S. Flag Steamer "Benton."
Off Memphis. June 6th 1862.

Sir:

I have respectfully to request that you will surrender the City of Memphis to the authority of the United States which I have the honor to represent.

I am, Mr. Mayor,
with high respect.
Your most Obt. Servt.
C. H. Davis
Flag Officer,
Commanding,
&c. &c. &c.

To his Honor,
The Mayor of the City of Memphis,
Tenn.

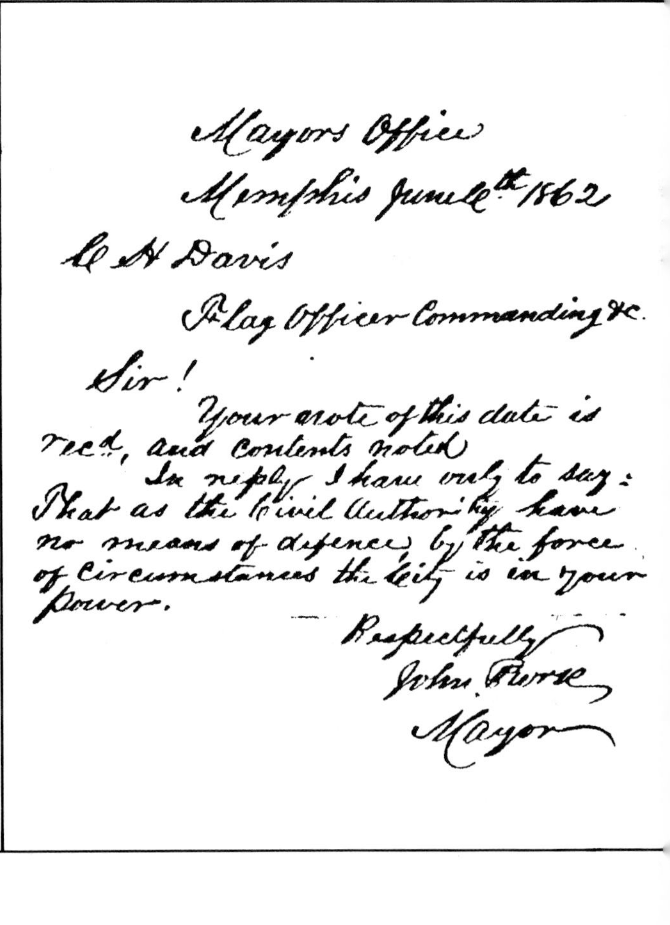
Mayors Office
Memphis June 6th 1862

C H Davis
Flag Officer Commanding &c.

Sir!

Your note of this date is recd, and contents noted
In reply I have only to say: That as the Civil Authority have no means of defence, by the force of circumstances the City is in your power.

Respectfully
John Park
Mayor

Thompson, the *Bragg* and the *Sumter* were shelled into burning masses. By 7:00 A.M. every Southern boat except one had been captured, sunk or damaged beyond repair; only the *Van Dorn* had eluded her pursuers and escaped downstream.

During the hour-and-a-half Battle of Memphis, the Confederates lost seven boats and 88 men killed or wounded. The only serious Union casualty was Colonel Ellet, who died two weeks later. He was buried as a hero, with his funeral service held at Independence Hall in Philadelphia.

Unable to offer any resistance to the Union landing parties, Memphis surrendered. One of Colonel Ellet's officers asked Mayor John Park to turn over the city, and sadly the Mayor agreed. A Southern sympathizer fired a single shot in anger when a Union soldier began replacing the Confederate flag at the city's post office at Third and Jefferson Streets with the Stars and Stripes.

Memphis and all its citizens were now under Northern control. For the duration of the war, Memphis would remain a conquered city. The Mississippi River was now open all the way to Vicksburg, and General Grant moved into Memphis to plan his campaign to take this last remaining Confederate fortress on the Mississippi River.

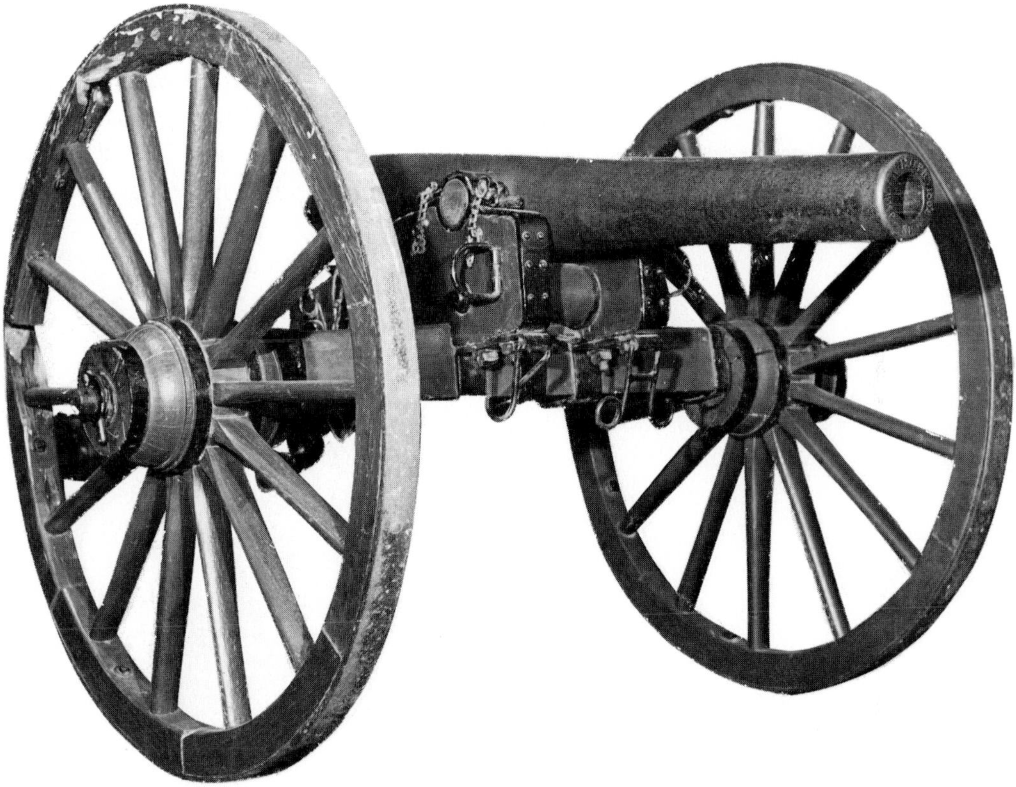

3-INCH FIELD PIECE

This 3-inch wrought iron rifled cannon is number 120 of a model developed and made by the Phoenix Iron Company of Phoenixville, Pennsylvania. In addition to the number and manufacturer's initials, the date, 1862, and weight, 813 (or 815), are stamped on the muzzle mouth. Unusual among such field pieces existing today is the original wooden carriage on this one, still in excellent condition. Such muzzle-loaded cannon were among the most popular field guns of both Confederate and Union artillerymen. Three inches was the diameter of the projectile inserted in the barrel.

CHAPTER 4

Conquered City

WHEN THE Indiana troops under Colonel G. N. Fitch took possession of Memphis, they quickly discovered that only the city had been conquered, not its citizens. For hours after Mayor John Park surrendered Memphis, the Bonnie Blue Flag of the Confederacy continued to wave with taunting insolence over the heads of the blue-clad invaders. Not until the afternoon of June 6, 1862, were Federal soldiers able to remove the last Confederate flag, which had been nailed to a flagstaff above the corner of Jefferson and Front Streets.

For weeks Memphians had been afraid the city would soon fall into enemy hands. They had felt the full

POST OFFICE FLAG
Reportedly this Confederate flag was taken by Union troops from the Memphis Post Office flag staff on June 6, 1862.

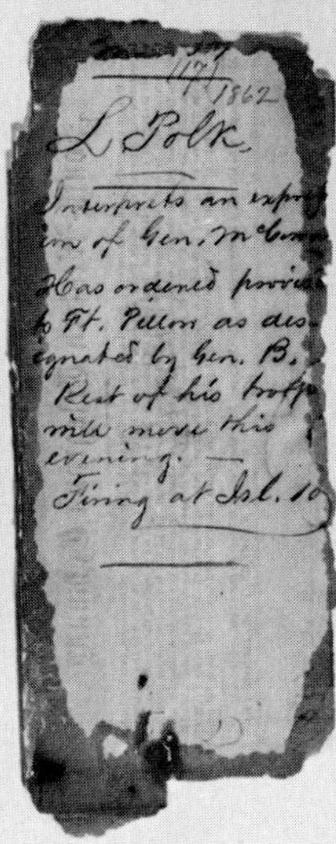

(LEFT)

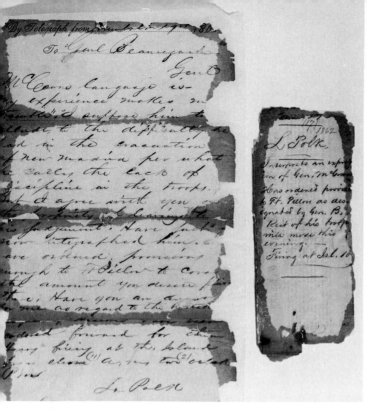

By Telegraph from Humbolt, 17th, 186...

To Genl Beauregard

Genl. McCowns language is . . . my experience makes me tremble. I suppose him to allude to the difficulty he had in the evacuation of New Madrid per (sic) what he calls the lack of discipline in the troops. But I agree with you in the propriety of leaving to his judgement. Have just telegraphed him. I have ordered provisions enough to Ft. Pillow to cover the amount you desire . . . these. Have you an answer for me as regard . . . been ordered forward for them. Heavy firing at the Island from eleven (11) A. M. two (2) o'clock P.M.

L. Polk

(RIGHT)

March 17, 1862

L. Polk,

Interperts an expression of Gen. McCown. Has ordered provisions to Ft. Pillow as designated by Gen. B. Rest of his troops move this evening.

Firing at Isl. 10.

CONFEDERATE TELEGRAMS
The telegraph was used during the Civil War for the first time as an integral part of military communication. From Humbolt, Tennessee, CSA General Polk sent this message to CSA General Beauregard. The "Genl McCown" mentioned was Confederate General John P. McCown, commander of the fortifications on Island No. 10 (tenth in series of Mississippi River islands counting southward from the mouth of the Ohio River). Fort Pillow, 40 miles north of Memphis, was a major Confederate river fortification. Island No. 10 fell April April 7, 1862 after being under heavy attack from Federal land and river forces and Fort Pillow was captured the day before the Battle of Memphis.

weight of their jeopardy when Governor Isham Harris and the legislature ended Memphis' brief period as Tennessee's capital and fled south with all the state's records.

Their anxiety for the city's fate had begun with the fall of Nashville, the first Confederate capital to fall into Union hands, and continued to grow as Confederate wounded streamed into Memphis from Shiloh, Island Number 10 and Corinth. Every available hospital bed was filled, and the remaining wounded were placed in hotels and private homes. Among those broken and bleeding from battle wounds suffered at Shiloh was Bedford Forrest. For 21 days his gentle Mary Ann nursed the wound, caused by a rifle ball which had torn the big muscles of his back and lodged close to the spinal column.

Forrest had been wounded the day after he feared his son, Willie, had become a Shiloh casualty. Most of the night of April 6, Forrest had searched among the moaning and screaming wounded without finding his son. He later learned that 15-year-old Willie and two companions, the son of Episcopal Bishop James Hervey Otey and the son of General Daniel S. Donelson, had reported with a handful of Yankee stragglers they had captured.

Throughout May, gray-clad soldiers under General P. G. T. Beauregard prepared for the military evacuation of Memphis. They packed up all machinery for making guns and ammunition, the stores of the quartermaster and ordnance departments, and even the contents of dry goods and clothing stores. Nothing was to be left behind that would benefit the enemy. What could not be carried away with the departing troops was destroyed.

Although the Federal occupation force found a few loyal Unionists and some neutral foreign immigrants willing to affirm their allegiance to the Union, the majority of the populace, comprised of women, Confederate wounded and men either too young or too old for

WOUNDED IN WAGON
At the end of the long, jolting wagon ride to Memphis, many Confederate casualties from the Shiloh and Corinth battlefields had to wait until an overworked medical staff could provide treatment.

JACKSON'S MONUMENT AT MEMPHIS, TENNESSEE, DEFACED BY THE REBELS (Sketched by Alexander Simplot)
A not-so-passive act of defiance to Union occupation was the defacing of the north side of the Jackson monument on which was carved: "The Federal Union It Must And Shall Be Preserved." Harper's Weekly *reported July 5, 1862, that "the word 'Federal' and the first two letters of 'Union' have been chipped by some rampant rebel, presenting an appearance as if a small hammer had been several times struck across the obnoxious words. It was a very feeble attempt at defacement of the words that grated harshly on treason's ear."* (Harper's Weekly)

military service, still had an unquenched spirit of rebellion.

The very day this city passed into Federal hands, the citizens initiated passive resistance, with businesses remaining unopened and the city's government unattended. They were encouraged by the "seditious" editorials in the *Avalanche* until Federal authorities took over the pressroom and banished editor Matt Gallaway from the city. Fanny Gallaway soon followed her husband south. She tore the Stars and Stripes from the gate of her confiscated home on Madison Avenue and was ordered to leave Memphis.

ULYSSES S. GRANT
Grant was commanding general of Union forces in the West from the fall of 1861 to the spring of 1864, when he became commander of all Union forces.

In July 1862 General Grant took personal command of the city and attempted to placate its citizens. He succeeded admirably in earning the respect of Elizabeth Meriwether in her dispute with a Mrs. Hickey. The detached summer kitchen of the Meriwether home on the outskirts of the city had been summarily taken over by Mrs. Hickey and was being operated as a saloon for Union soldiers of the nearby picket or guard camp. Although she was the wife of a Confederate officer, Elizabeth Meriwether was advised by a friendly Union soldier to take her case to General Grant. Accompanied by the soldier, she went to General Grant's headquarters in the William Richardson Hunt mansion on Beale Street and was ushered into the parlor to await Grant's summons. When she was escorted into his presence, he was seated

HUNT (PHELAN) HOUSE
The Hunt House served as Grant's headquarters and residence while he was in Memphis. It had formerly been the home of William and Julia Hunt but was confiscated because of Colonel Hunt's ordnance service for the Confederacy.

at a table, an unlit cigar in his mouth. Without expression Grant listened to Mrs. Meriwether's story, then wrote a few words on a piece of paper which he handed to her with a gruff "Take that to the Provost Marshal." The note brought an end to Mrs. Hickey's saloon.

General Alvin P. Hovey succeeded Grant as the city's commandant. He made few friends when he ordered all males 18 to 45 to sign the Union loyalty oath or leave town. Over 1,300 men chose to join the Confederate army rather than submit, thereby adding to the Rebel ranks.

When General William T. Sherman took over from Hovey in July 1862, he found the stores, schools and churches still closed and the municipal government not functioning. In an effort to get things moving again, he rescinded Hovey's loyalty order, allowed trade without passes over the five roads leading into the city and lectured Mayor Park on his civil duties. Sherman also increased the police force from 32 to 100 officers. The additional cost was to be met by a saloon and bordello tax. The police were put under the control of the Provost Marshal who now had his headquarters in the Irvin Block (popularly called Irving Block), which had been converted from a Confederate hospital into a military and civilian prison.

Sherman attempted to guide the rebellious citizenry back into the Union not only in the streets and homes but in the churches as well. Attending services at Cavalry Episcopal Church with his staff, Sherman ordered the minister to include in his prayer a petition for the divine protection of President Lincoln or the church would be closed. The minister complied. The congregation of the Second Presbyterian Church at Main and Beale was turned out of its elegant building because it had offered the church bell for Confederate cannon. The building was renamed the Union Chapel and provided nondenominational services for convalescent Federal soldiers and later became the first Freedmen's School.

Disloyalty enraged Sherman and caused him to be

WILLIAM TECUMSEH SHERMAN
Sherman was the most disliked of the commandants of Memphis during the Union occupation.

harsher than was necessary in carrying out Grant's instructions to banish all disloyal families from the city and to confiscate rents and all vacant stores as well as residences belonging to disloyal persons. He was irritated by the partisan bands that roamed the countryside, raiding the city's suburbs and making it dangerous for Federal soldiers to walk alone at night. These guerillas also shot at river transports and the coaches of the Memphis & Charleston Railroad. In retaliation, Sherman ordered Memphians to sit by the windows of the train to be the next targets. As an object lesson he burned

GUERILLA SHARPSHOOTERS
Partisan bands operated freely around Memphis until the close of the war.

Randolph, once Memphis' rival for river supremacy, to the ground the day after partisans fired at Union boats.

Sherman's Special Order # 254 provided for the expulsion of ten Memphis families every time a boat was fired upon. In November 1862 Elizabeth Meriwether's family was among the first Sherman ordered to leave. She was then eight months pregnant and had two small boys, ages 3 and 5. She aroused Sherman's ire by protesting the confiscation of rents from property in her name. When she pleaded for a delay because of her advanced pregnancy, she was given the choice of leaving Memphis within 24 hours or being incarcerated in the Irving Block prison for the duration of the war. This infamous Federal prison, which housed both Confederate soldiers and male and female citizens, was such a place of horror that it was ultimately ordered investigated by President Lincoln and closed. Unfortunately the cruel and nightmarish treatment had already caused the deaths of some whose only crime had been attempting to smuggle medicine to a sick son or uniform cloth to a sweetheart.

Elizabeth Meriwether had no choice but to load her Rockaway carriage with all the possessions she could carry, bundle her two sons, Avery and Rivers, in warm clothing and blankets and set off with her mule, Adrienne. It was a dismal journey through a countryside

FLIGHT OF ELIZABETH MERIWETHER
This gallant Southern lady courageously faced Sherman and was expelled from Memphis although she was eight months pregnant. She managed to carry her family to safety with the help of her faithful mule, "Adrienne."

stark with approaching winter and desolated by war. For over a month she sought safety and shelter, braving cold rains and muddy roads. She found shelter at night in isolated cabins, where she shared meager suppers with the inhabitants, until she reached Columbus, Mississippi. There, on Christmas Eve 1862, she found refuge in the home of Mrs. Rebecca Winston, just in time to give birth to a third son, whom she named Lee after the Confederate general.

When Federal troops were reported moving toward Columbus, Elizabeth Meriwether hitched the mule to the Rockaway and again set out, with her baby and two young sons. Moving from place to place for the next two and a half years, she roamed the South like a vagabond, just one step ahead of the constantly advancing Union army.

There were few "disloyal" citizens left in Memphis, or at least few who let their sympathies for the South be known. A rapacious horde of profiteers, prostitutes, blockade runners and unscrupulous merchants boosted the depleted population to 40,000, three-fourths of whom could number their length of residence in months or weeks. They started arriving as soon as trading in cotton behind Union lines was endorsed by the Secretary of the Treasury. Cotton was then worth $300 a bale in gold, and that meant a 20-cent profit per pound for cotton delivered to textile mills in the North.

The Assistant Secretary of War, C. S. Dana, was alarmed by the cotton trade in Memphis. Dana said, "Every colonel, captain and quartermaster is in secret partnership with some operation in cotton; while every soldier dreams of adding a bale to his monthly pay. . . ."

This insatiable greed for cotton produced an inflationary spiral, causing the price to soar from 13 cents a pound in 1860 to $1.44 a pound by war's end. Cotton also made Memphis the contraband capital for the Confederate army. It is estimated that between $30 million and $40 million worth of military goods reached the Confederacy through Memphis.

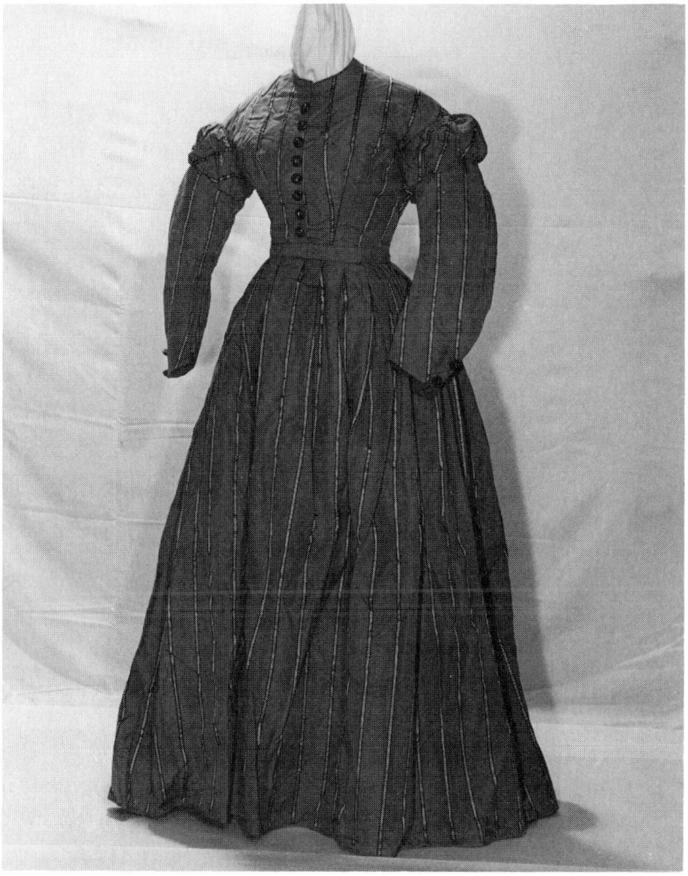

LIBERTY HEAD DRESS
The woman who wore this dress was undoubtedly the wife of a Union sympathizer. The dress is made of heavy linen and has Liberty Head buttons prominently displayed on the front.

LIBERTY HEAD BUTTONS

Although this influx of gold inflated prices in Memphis, the steadily depreciating currency of the Confederacy created an unbelievable inflationary crisis by 1863. In her memoirs Mrs. Jefferson Davis wrote that in Richmond in February 1863 the price for bacon was $6 a pound, ham $7 a pound and turkeys $60 each. In Tuscaloosa, Alabama, at the end of 1863, Elizabeth Meriwether found a barrel of flour cost $600, sugar was $30 a pound, a ham was $300, and a turkey was now $175.

By April 1, 1864, the cost of goods in the South had skyrocketed to the point that it took 75 Confederate dollars to buy a bushel of beans; tea was $22 a pound; coffee, $12 a pound; and milk was $4 a quart. As the war neared its end in 1865, a haircut and shave cost $10, a suit of men's clothes was $2,700, and one yard of linen cloth cost 200 Confederate dollars. It took $1,700

CLOTH AND CONFEDERATE MONEY
The dress material was purchased in Charleston, South Carolina, during the war for $60 per yard. The cost of an entire dress was $720 in Confederate paper money.

to purchase one ounce of quinine and $50 in Confederate bills for one bar of Windsor soap.

One year after the fall of Memphis, the Union still had not been able to gain complete control of the Mississippi. On July 15, 1862, the giant Memphis-built ram, *Arkansas*, had defeated the combined force of Union gunboats *Carondolet*, *Tyler* and *Queen of the West* and had managed to slip past the whole Union fleet below Vicksburg, finally taking refuge under the city's batteries. The Confederate ram had been towed safely out of Memphis a month earlier before the city fell and hurriedly outfitted on the Yazoo River. On July 22 Union Commodore Farragut risked his whole fleet in an attempt to destroy the *Arkansas*, moored at the Vicksburg waterfront, but failed in his mission. A second attempt by the Union boats *Essex* and *Queen of the West*, now commanded by Lieutenant Colonel Alfred W. Ellet, the ship designer's brother, also suffered defeat. Not until August 6 did the *Arkansas* succumb to the fortunes of war when it was destroyed at Baton Rouge, Louisiana, by its own crew to avoid capture.

During April and May of 1863, Grant's forces had

RE-ENFORCEMENTS FOR GRANT'S ARMY LEAVING MEMPHIS, TENNESSEE
"Our sketch shows the Alice Dean, *a crack Western steamer, leaving Memphis with re-enforcements, and with doctors, nurses, etc., for the wounded. She was in charge of the Cincinnati branch of the United States Sanitary Commission, and commanded by Mr. R. B. Moore, of Cincinnati. She was a very fast boat, having run up to Cincinnati from Memphis in 2 days, 23 hours and 5 minutes. The scene depicted was one of constant occurrence, as troops were pouring daily into Memphis from all parts."* (Harper's Weekly, *1862*)

failed to take Vicksburg, the last large Confederate bastion on the Mississippi, in spite of repeated attempts. A natural fortress, Vicksburg was perched high upon a bluff commanding the river and was almost unapproachable from the north or northeast because of streams and swamps. Since Vicksburg could not be taken by assault, Grant's army had encircled the entrenched Confederates commanded by General John C. Pemberton and settled down to a siege that would starve the defenders into surrender.

Even though Grant's forces were supported by a gunboat flotilla, they were blocked in every attempt to take Vicksburg by the stiff and stubborn resistance of Rebel troops. Reinforcements had to be sent in to replace Grant's heavy battle losses and deaths from malaria and smallpox. Finally, on July 4, the 30,000 starving Confederates surrendered, and the emaciated

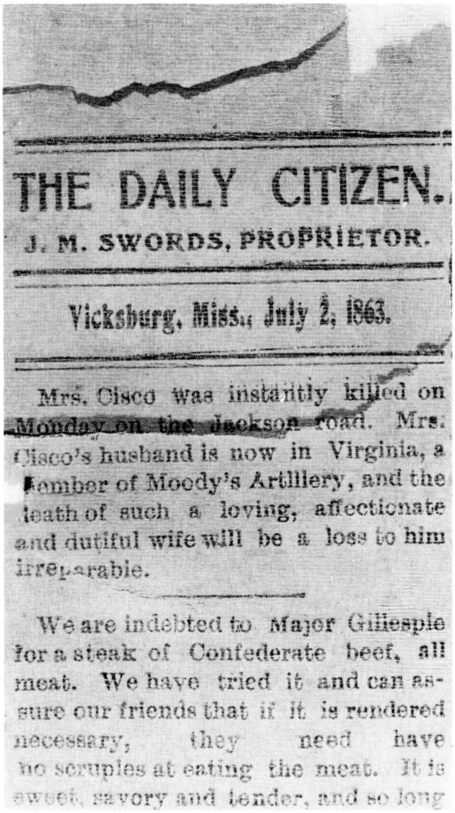
THE DAILY CITIZEN.

J. M. SWORDS, PROPRIETOR.

Vicksburg, Miss., July 2, 1863.

Mrs. Cisco was instantly killed on Monday on the Jackson road. Mrs. Cisco's husband is now in Virginia, a member of Moody's Artillery, and the death of such a loving, affectionate and dutiful wife will be a loss to him irreparable.

We are indebted to Major Gillespie for a steak of Confederate beef, all meat. We have tried it and can assure our friends that if it is rendered necessary, they need have no scruples at eating the meat. It is sweet, savory and tender, and so long

DAILY CITIZEN *OF VICKSBURG*
This newspaper, printed on wallpaper two days before Vicksburg's surrender, is a rare example of the citizens' stubborn courage in spite of great hardships and suffering.

civilian survivors crawled from their caves in the hillside, listened in awe to the silence and stared at the battered ruins of what was left of their homes and shops.

While Grant's forces were camped in front of Vicksburg, the former Memphis alderman, slave trader and plantation owner, Nathan Bedford Forrest, was beginning to display the brilliant cavalry tactics that would earn him the accolades of "Wizard in the Saddle" and "That Devil Forrest." In the judgment of historian Bruce Catton, Forrest was "one of the authentic military geniuses of the whole war. If they could have caught him (at Fort Donelson) and kept him under lock and key to the end of the war, the Federals would have saved themselves much anguish."

Anguish is exactly what Forrest tried to give the Union commanders, and he usually succeeded. In his home country of western Tennessee and northern Mississippi, Forrest displayed such constant brilliance in overcoming superior numbers that he became the special target of forces sent against him by the Union commanders in Memphis.

All of Forrest's raids had certain common aims: to smash Federal supply and communication lines, especially the railroads that connected Memphis with the North; and to interfere with Union plans elsewhere in the South. He also made the enemy his quartermaster for he supplied his regiment by capturing Union provisions, munitions and horses.

The Union commanders at Memphis desperately wanted to capture or destroy Forrest and his troops. Martial law was declared in Memphis on July 2, 1864 by General Washburn as part of an effort to prevent Confederate sympathizers from providing aid and information to Forrest. A concentrated Union effort to defeat Forrest and take northern Mississippi had begun during June 1864, when General Samuel D. Sturgis left Memphis with 8,000 soldiers, a large number of cannon and sufficient supplies for an extended campaign. Forrest met Sturgis at Brice's Cross Roads, near Guntown, Mississippi, with a force half the size of Sturgis'. He completely routed the Union army in a fierce encounter that left 2,000 Union casualties. Sturgis lost not only a quarter of his army but all his artillery and most of his supply wagons.

General Sherman was outraged by this defeat and ordered another expedition against Forrest's home ground. A new force of 14,000 men was led by Generals Andrew J. Smith and Joseph R. Mower. On July 14 this force collided with General S. D. Lee's 9,000 Confederates at Tupelo and, in spite of soundly defeating the Southern force, the cautious General Smith withdrew his force to Memphis.

Smith assembled another force of 18,000 men and left Memphis in search of Forrest on August 1, 1864. In moving carefully toward Oxford, Mississippi, Smith was

DOLL HAT
Martial law was clamped so tightly on Memphis that even a doll's hat was scrutinized. The hat was made by the wife of Major Phil Allen of the Confederate army and sent through the Union lines to Mrs. Allen's niece. The Union pickets are reported to have said, "Let it pass. It is as frail as the Confederacy."

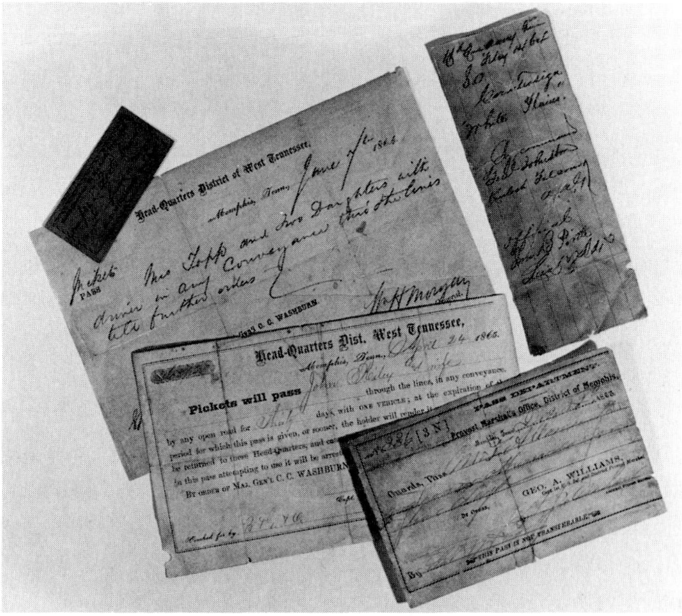

MILITARY PASSES
Martial law and military jurisdiction meant that even civilians had to have passes to move from one area to another.

blocked by 2,000 of Forrest's men under the command of General James R. Chalmers. Forrest, with an additional 2,000 men, outflanked Smith and raided Memphis on August 21, 1864. Forrest's objective was twofold: he hoped to capture Generals Stephen S. Hurlburt and Cadwallader C. Washburn as well as to threaten Smith's lines of communication and supply and cause him to withdraw from Mississippi. Forrest failed to capture the Union generals, but he achieved his other objective when Smith pulled back to Memphis.

The raid on Memphis began early on a foggy Sunday morning and had as its primary objectives the Gayoso House where General Hurlburt was quartered and the headquarters of General Washburn on Union Avenue and Third Street. However, as neither general was at

GENERAL WASHBURN
Commandant of Memphis at the time Forrest raided the city, Washburn is said to have fled in his nightshirt to escape Forrest's troopers.

FORREST'S RAID INTO MEMPHIS – THE REBELS AT THE GAYOSO HOUSE
(Sketched by George H. Ellsbury)
The Gayoso House was the hotel where Union General Hurlbut, as well as many other Federal officers and civilian officials, stayed while in Memphis. (Harper's Weekly)

home at the time of the attack, both escaped capture. While some of Forrest's men were looking for the generals, another detachment became involved in a brisk but brief battle at the State Female College, which persuaded Forrest to withdraw his troops before they were trapped in the city.

When Forrest left Memphis, he took 400 captured horses and 600 prisoners with him. He also left town with General Washburn's full-dress uniform. Later, when the prisoners were exchanged, Washburn's uniform was returned to him. Washburn gallantly ordered a brand new Confederate uniform, to be made by Forrest's own Memphis tailor and sent through the lines to Forrest. This was still the age of chivalry.

FORREST'S RAID INTO MEMPHIS – REBEL ATTACK ON THE IRVING PRISON
(Sketched by George H. Ellsbury)
One of Forrest's detachments made a vain attempt to break past the Union guards and free friends and families imprisoned within these hated walls. (Harper's Weekly)

One incident earlier in 1864 ruined General Forrest's reputation with Northerners. On April 12, 1864, his detachment attacked the Union-held Fort Pillow, Tennessee (40 miles north of Memphis), garrisoned by a black infantry regiment and a detachment of loyalist Tennessee cavalry. Of the 557 soldiers (about half of them black troops), almost 400 were killed, wounded or captured. One of Forrest's troopers, Alex Jones, wrote this hasty after-battle account to his wife, Sallie:

" . . . arriving at Fort Pillow a little after sun rise

(we) captured the pickets. Fussell's Co. the company I was acting with was thrown as scrimishers after advancing about half mile we came in view of their outer fortifications and drove them back into their fort. The regiment coming up about then we commensed fighting and advancing slowly taking advantage of the ground as we moved up placing out sharpshooters to keep their

THE MASSACRE AT FORT PILLOW
Poor judgment on the part of the part of the Union commander at Fort Pillow resulted in heavy casualties. The term "massacre" was used by Northern newspapers as war propaganda and as Republican election material. (Harper's Weekly)

HOTCHKISS SHELL
The Hotchkiss explosive projectile, made by Hotchkiss and Sons of New York, was one of the principle types of field ammunition used during the Civil War. Various calibers up to 12 inches were produced. This 3-inch shell, dug from the river bank at Memphis, is apparently a Confederate copy since it lacks the patent markings of U.S. ordnance.

heads down when we had to pass exposed points. Moving up in that way until we got within twenty steps of the fort when there was a flag sent in demanding a surrender. They refused unless we would treat the Nigroes as prisoners of war which we refused to do that we would have to hold them for exchange then we were ordered to charge the fort. When the work of death commenced them inside and we a vaulting up the embankment on the outside fighting . . . our guns together killing and capturing every man in the place. The exact number I have not been able to learn. Between two and three hundred I think our loss I learn was 28 killed."

The high loss of life was due to the decision of Major Lionel F. Booth (6th United States Heavy Artillery) to fight rather than surrender, even though he was outnumbered and surrounded. Major Booth believed he could retreat from the redoubt and be protected by the cannon of the gunboats on the river; the gunboats, however, failed to render support and moved out of range once the guns of the fort were captured by the Confederates and turned toward the river.

The term "massacre" was first applied to the battle at Fort Pillow in a report by the Union Congressional Committee on the Conduct of the War and was used in Republican Party campaign literature, encouraging people to vote the Republican ticket in the 1864 Presidential election.

Forrest's raid into Memphis was the one bright spot for Southern sympathizers living there, and it would live in their memories along with the bitter experiences of the Union occupation of their city.

GENERAL OFFICER'S MOUNT
The Memphis raid by Forrest allowed him to remount some of his troopers with captured Union horses.

Mrs. Amelia Hill Freeman
These ladies with Mrs. J.J. Hill of
Tupelo Mississippi made this flag
which Mrs. Ella Gardner Smith (left)
presented to General Nathan Bedford
Forrest - Commander of the second
Tennessee Cavalry Corps in the
Autumn of 1862
Presented by Tupelo Chapter UDC
Mrs. Ella Gardner Smith
Mrs. Annie Wiley Frazer

FORREST BATTLE FLAG

Mrs. Ella Gardner Smith, Mrs. Amelia Hill Freeman, Mrs. Annie Wiley Frazer and Mrs. J. J. Hill of Tupelo, Mississippi, presented a corps flag to General Nathan Bedford Forrest, commander of the Second Tennessee Cavalry Corps, in the autumn of 1862. The handmade battle flag is supposed to have been captured by Union forces in Memphis at the site of the State Female College on McLemore Avenue on August 21, 1864, during the Forrest raid.

KATE MAGEVNEY
Kate Mageveney, the youngest daughter of the former Memphis schoolmaster, Eugene Magevney, married John Dawson in 1867. (Courtesy of St. Peter's Catholic Church, Memphis)

CHAPTER 5

An Impoverished Peace

THE BOOMING of cannons, the rattle of musket fire and the anguished screams of wounded and dying soldiers finally ended in April 1865. Throughout the South Confederate armies surrendered; the war was over. Now the men in the blue and the gray could go home.

Home to Sallie and the "cute little cubs" in Madison County went trooper Alex Jones; home to Memphis and his bride-to-be, Kate Magevney, went Lieutenant Colonel John Dawson; home to Bolivar to open a new school in the abandoned railway station went Private (soon professor) John Hubbard; home to Mary Ann went General Forrest on King Phillip, his dapple-gray stallion; home to Mother went the 19-year-old veteran Willie Forrest; and home came Elizabeth and Colonel Minor Meriwether with their three sons, who hardly knew what a home was. But there were some, like those aboard the steamboat *Sultana*, who would never come home.

The steamboat *Sultana* left New Orleans for Cairo, Illinois, on April 21, 1865. Designed to carry 376 passengers, she left New Orleans with only 100 passengers and 80 crewmen. Her first major stop was Vicksburg, Mississippi. Vicksburg was being used as a shipping depot for former Union prisoners, many of whom had been liberated from the infamous Andersonville camp in Georgia. These men were being sent north 1,000 at a time as steamboats became available. The *Henry Ames* with 1,300 men and the *Olive Branch* with 700 left Vicksburg just before the *Sultana* docked. A rumor spread among the freed prisoners that a Union officer was receiving a bribe to put the men on boats owned by a certain company. The officer in charge of transporting

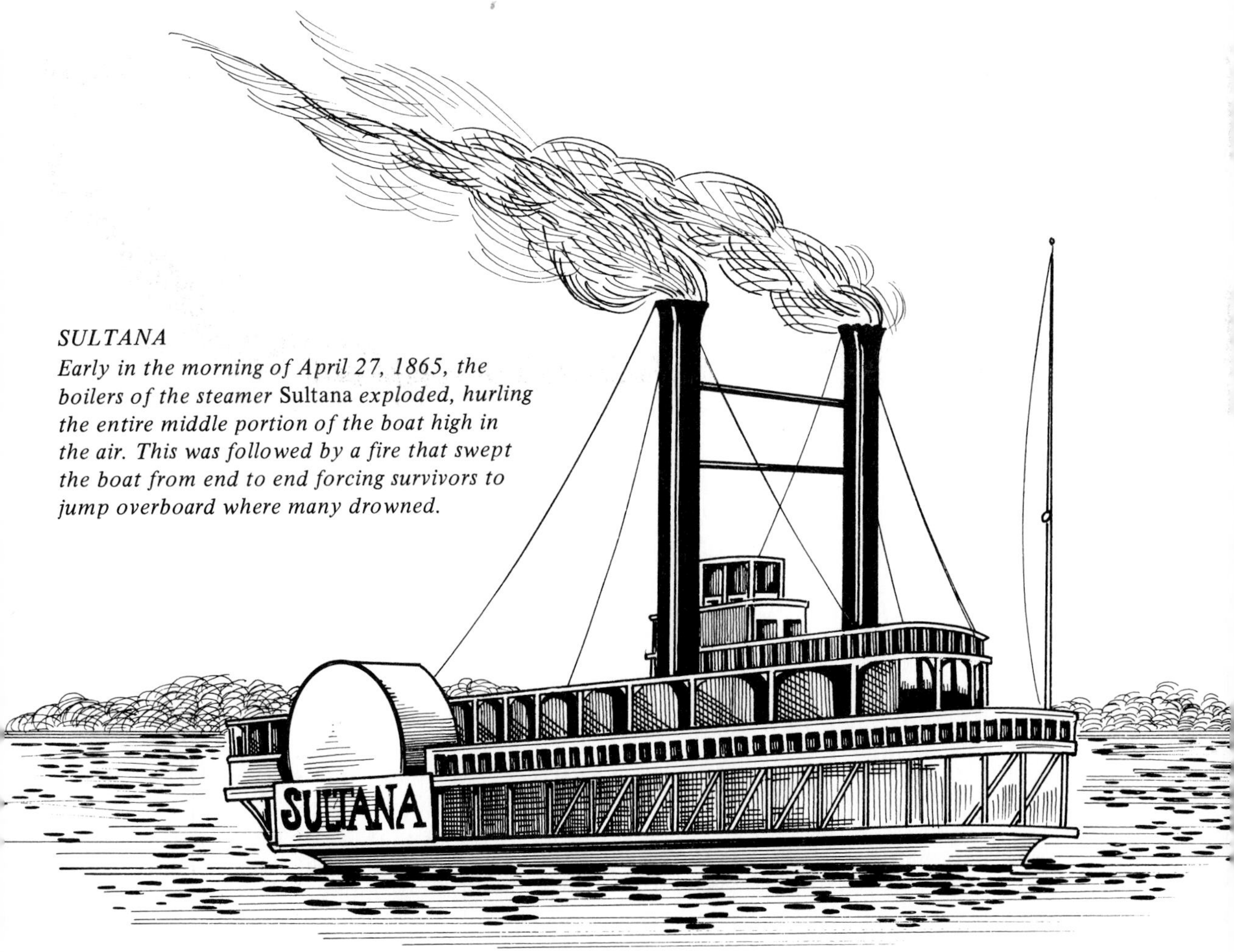

SULTANA

Early in the morning of April 27, 1865, the boilers of the steamer Sultana *exploded, hurling the entire middle portion of the boat high in the air. This was followed by a fire that swept the boat from end to end forcing survivors to jump overboard where many drowned.*

the former prisoners decided to load all the remaining men aboard the *Sultana* to squelch the rumor. An exact count was not kept, but one Union officer said there were no fewer than 2,400 soldiers and 180 civilians crammed bow to stern.

The *Sultana* labored for 18 hours in the flood-swollen current to make the trip to Memphis, arriving there at 7 A.M. She remained in Memphis long enough to unload some cargo and to refuel, then left the city about 2 P.M., headed for Cairo. Seven miles upstream her overburdened boilers blew up, scalding numerous soldiers and sending iron splinters into others. Immediately the boat burst into flames and began to drift aimlessly in the current.

Those who had not been blown into the river began

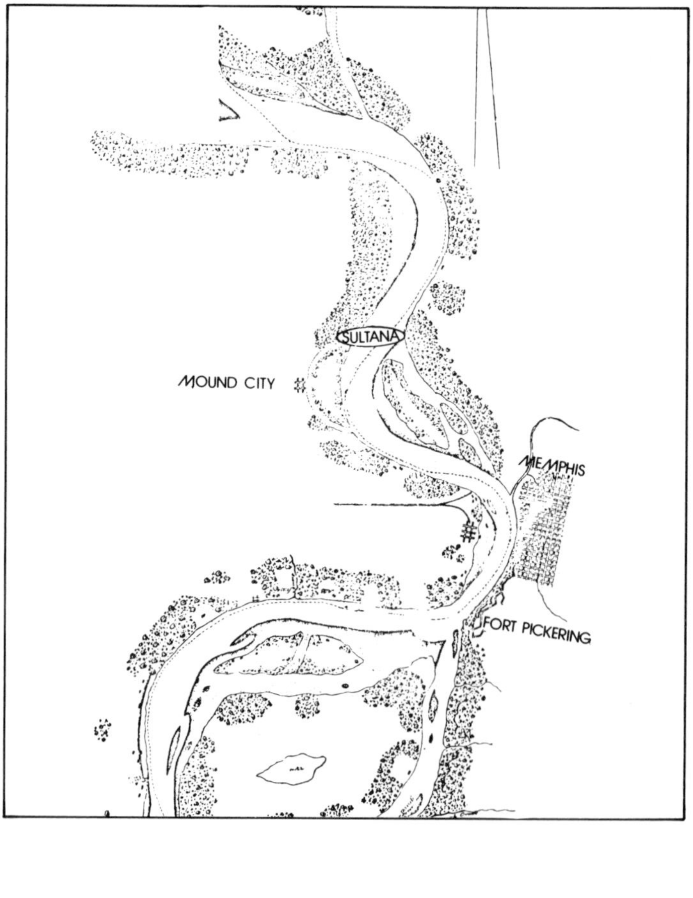

SULTANA EXPLOSION SITE
The explosion occurred midstream, a mile from land on either side. The flaming mass of the once-fine steamer drifted down with the current and sank in about 20 feet of water near the Arkansas shore. For many years after the boat's jackstaff was visible above the water, marking the site of the worst maritime disaster in history.

to jump into the turbulent water to escape the leaping flames. Even the best swimmers, weakened by months of brutal captivity, could not struggle long against the current; many who might have been able to swim to safety were drowned by other clutching, frantic victims. A few were able to cling to pieces of wreckage until they were picked up. The *Bostonia* was the first boat on the scene and rescued about 100 survivors. Several boats arrived later and saved others. By morning, charred bodies of hundreds who had perished began floating past the Memphis riverfront. Of the almost 2,600 people on board the *Sultana*, only 800 lived. Even though this was the greatest marine disaster in history, topping by 30 the toll of the *Titanic*, the *New York Times* devoted only three inches of a single column to reporting the tragedy. The assassination of one man, President Abraham Lincoln, overshadowed the deaths of hundreds.

Memphians themselves were not affected by the *Sultana* disaster in spite of its huge loss of life. Other things concerned them more personally. One major concern of the freshly paroled Confederates was the large number of freed slaves now in the city. From a black population of fewer than 4,000, there were now nearly 15,000 blacks living in the city.

Before the Civil War the black population of Memphis was only about 15 percent of the whole, and most of these were household servants who lived in their own quarters behind the house of their master. Others who were skilled at a trade, such as carpenters, were hired out to work for a contractor in the city and often led a semi-independent existence. Freedmen were few (about 200 in 1860), and they were outcasts in a slave-master society, looked down on by many of the slaves themselves, who were generally better housed, fed and clothed.

After Memphis' capture by the Union and Lincoln's Emancipation Proclamation, the city became a refuge for slaves from Mississippi and Arkansas. During the last three years of the war blacks flocked into South Memphis where Camp Fiske, the Union contraband camp, or

THE CAMP OF THE CONTRABANDS ON THE BANKS OF THE MISSISSIPPI, FORT PICKERING, MEMPHIS, TENN.
(Sketched by Henri Levin)
By 1865 the black population of Memphis had grown from less than 4,000 to over 15,000. Near the Union Fort Pickering was Camp Fiske, established for "contrabands," as masterless slaves were termed by the Federal commanders of Memphis. (Harper's Weekly)

holding camp for former slaves, offered freedom, log houses, churches, schools and marriage licenses with a flag of the United States printed on them.

Lincoln created the Freedmen's Bureau and put it under the direction of the War Department to care for the thousands of blacks liberated from slavery. The Bureau was to feed, clothe and educate these former slaves. It also acted as a federal arbiter between white employers and black workers, arranging contracts which stipulated wages and working conditions.

In Memphis the Freedman's Bureau focused on education. The first school formed for the freed slaves in early 1863 was in a barrack building in South Memphis and was headed by Fannie Kiddo. In October 1864 L. H. Cobb was appointed superintendent of black schools in Memphis, and one of the very early black leaders and teachers in the freedmen's schools was Joseph Clouston. By 1865, 22 schools for blacks had been established with an enrollment of 1,101 students.

Captain J. A. Walker, the Superintendent of Contrabands, under the overall command of Colonel John Eaton Jr., the General Superintendent of the Freedmen's Bureau for West Tennessee, had a difficult time getting the Bureau to run smoothly. In his report for March 1864 Walker said:

"Since I entered upon the duties of my present position, many of the detailed men have been relieved, and whilst I have had the cheerful cooperation of most of those connected with the department, some of them have proved very inefficient and others, not appreciating

FREEDMEN'S SCHOOL
The Freedmen's Bureau was created to provide for the liberated slaves' welfare and education.

the importance of punctuality and system, have signally failed in the most reasonable requirement."

Not all blacks in the city were living in the contraband camps. There were some who had been freed years before the Civil War and had their own homes and businesses in the Beale Street area. There were also four regiments of Negro troops stationed at Fort Pickering, and relations between blacks and whites had been strained by incidents between the races. The tense atmosphere was further heightened by poor economic conditions and a fierce, aggressive competition for jobs between the Irish and the blacks.

The black troops at Fort Pickering were required to patrol the city and were constantly in contact with Memphis' predominantly Irish police force. The blacks felt the police used unduly harsh methods in arresting "Negroes" and were angered by this mistreatment of members of their race. The community mood was like a bomb waiting for someone to light the fuse. In the spring of 1866 the match was struck. Four thousand Negro troops stationed at the fort were released from duty. Idleness and alcohol led a few of the freshly discharged soldiers to assault and harass poor whites in the area of the fort. On May 1, 1866, the bomb exploded when a small group of these soldiers attempted to prevent several Irish policemen from arresting a black man in South Memphis. The Memphis police force of 180 men, of which 167 were Irish, the fire department and the white rabble of the city rushed to South Memphis, where they indiscriminately slaughtered and burned in the black community. Federal troops temporarily restored order that evening, but the rioting broke out again the next morning and continued for two more days before Federal troops finally quelled the mob. When the fighting ceased, 44 blacks and two whites had been killed and another 75 people wounded. The rioting and burning cost black citizens 91 houses, four churches and 12 schools.

Radical Republicans used the Memphis riot to win the Congressional elections of November 1866 and

BLACK TROOPS
The North used black soldiers primarily as garrison or occupation troops because they were more responsive to discipline and desertion was unknown. However, black line units such as the 36th U.S. Colored Infantry achieved fame as fighters during the Virginia campaigns. Toward the close of the war there were 178,895 black soldiers serving in the Union Army.

defeat the lenient reconstruction plans of President Andrew Johnson as they were presented to Congress. The Northern papers, fired by Radical Republicans' rhetoric, charged Memphis with gross discrimination and murder. However, the city's newspapers and its decent citizenry cried out against the brutal and savage acts of those involved. Little was said in the North of the more numerous paroled Confederates who protected blacks by taking them into their homes during the rioting.

The explosive emotions after the riot, coupled with the shock of blacks who could vote and white disenfranchisement, led to the organization of the Ku Klux Klan. It was assumed by many that Nathan Bedford Forrest was its founder; however, this cannot be substantiated. Sources published long after Forrest's death said he was a member, as well as one of the organizers in Memphis, along with Matt Gallaway, Minor Meriwether and other prominent businessmen.

The "Invisible Empire," as the Ku Klux Klan became known, was originated by a half dozen young ex-Confederate soldiers in a little Middle Tennessee town in 1866. They held their meetings in a deserted and isolated house on the outskirts of town—reputed to be

**"We Regard The Revolution Acts (So Called) of Congress
As Usurpations, and Unconstitutional, Revolutionary, and Void." —
Democratic Platform**

POLITICAL CARTOON

A bloodthirsty Bedford Forrest, a wild-eyed white mob member and a Wall Street capitalist are united in subjugating a black Union soldier in this early Thomas Nast cartoon. Such emotional campaign tactics were used to discredit Horatio Seymour, the 1868 Democratic presidential candidate from New York, and to win support for the Republican candidate, U. S. Grant.

"haunted"—and soon word was being passed among superstitious blacks in the community that the ghosts of dead Confederates were meeting in the old house and marching around the countryside. Before long it was realized that the fears of rural blacks could become a weapon for the disenfranchised ex-Confederates against Reconstruction radicals who controlled the Negro vote.

The ghostly procession of men who "seemed to be an army" was a terrifying sight. Elizabeth Meriwether described them years later in her book, *Recollections of Ninety-Two Years*:

"It seemed to be an army of horses but the horses' feet did not make the usual noise and clatter. Their hoofs were wrapped in cloth, their bodies were covered with flowing white cotton cloth, their riders wore white hoods and white gowns which trailed almost to the ground. Hardly a sound did either horses or riders make—truly, in the light of that midnight moon, it did seem like an army of ghosts!"

The "ghosts" would stop by a black home and ask for a drink of water, which they drank by the bucketful, saying that was the best drink they had had since the Yankees shot them at Shiloh, and how the heat of hell had made them develop a monstrous thirst. The bucketfuls of water were poured down a tube by their throats and caught in waterproofed canvas bags concealed under the long flowing robes. These "ghosts" would then suggest the blacks not vote at the next election.

When the fanatical Governor William Brownlow and his Radical Republican supporters in the legislature lost control of Tennessee voters, Forrest felt the Klan had served its purpose and ordered it disbanded around 1869. Although the Klan continued in other Southern states, becoming a lawless terrorist group in some places, it came to an end in Memphis and in much of Tennessee. It was time to begin a true reconstruction.

MERIWETHER FAMILY—MINOR, ELIZABETH AND LEE (Age 3)
The Meriwether family, like so many families in the South, were finally reunited with the coming of peace.

"FLIGHT OF A WARRIOR'S SOUL"
The earliest known work of artist Carl Gutherz, this watercolor was reproduced as a print and postal card which was circulated throughout the Mid-South probably about 1865. Entitled "Flight of a Warrior's Soul" it shows angels carrying the battle-torn regimental flag of the 154th Senior Tennessee Infantry Regiment in which his brother, Frederick and other Memphians served. Carl won fame first as the creator of the Memphis Mardi Gras designs, and later earned national recognition for his talent.

CHAPTER 6

Rebuilding a City

AS THE last year of the decade began, Memphis was recovering from the effects of war, riot, financial panic and its second yellow fever epidemic. The resiliency of the city was being manifested in a renaissance of construction, commerce and culture.

The energetic Greenlaw brothers had built the $200,000 Greenlaw Opera House at the corner of Union and Second the first year after peace had been declared. It was a four-story brick building with a front featuring "classical porticoes" facing Second Street and an auditorium of 1,600 seats. Although most of the entertainment consisted of minstrel and vaudeville shows interspersed with temperance lectures and public meetings, performances were given by the Mozart Musical Society, which had its headquarters there. The building was also rented for the political gatherings of black Republicans, who were emerging as a voting force in local as well as national politics.

Most ex-Confederates were successfully rebuilding lives interrupted by war. Former Lieutenant Colonel

"MOTHER" JONES
Irish-born Mary Harris "Mother" Jones lost her husband and four children in the Memphis yellow fever epidemic of 1867, when 550 died. She lived 100 years (1830–1930) and became nationally recognized as a strong-willed leader of social reform. The magazine Mother Jones *was named after her.*

GENERAL VIEW OF THE CITY OF MEMPHIS, TENNESSEE, FROM HOPEFIELD, ON THE ARKANSAS SIDE (Harper's Weekly)

50 ADVERTISEMENTS.

WALKER BROS. & CO.,
Dealers in
FANCY AND STAPLE
DRY GOODS,
CLOTHING,
Boots, Shoes and Plantation Supplies,
No. 229 Main Street, CLAY BUILDING,
218 Front Street, corner Adams,
23 Jefferson St., next door Tennessee Nat. Bank,
MEMPHIS, TENNESSEE.

Having Our Own Clothing Manufactory,
No. 220 North Third St., PHILADELPHIA,
And Manufacturing exclusively for this Market, enables us to sell our Goods at Eas[illegible]

WALKER BROS. & CO.,
No. 229 Main St. (CLAY BUILDING.)

JOHN G. WALLACE. WM. P. [illegible]

JOHN G. WALLACE & CO.,
Commission Merchants,
AND WHOLESALE DEALERS IN
GROCERIES AND PLANTATION SUPPLIES,
No. 316 Front Street, between Union and Monroe, MEMPHIS, TENN.
LIBERAL CASH ADVANCES MADE ON COTTON.

THE CAPITAL SALOON,
Finley's Alley, Cor. Center Alley,
Between Front & Main, West Court & Madison Streets.
MEMPHIS, TENNESSEE.

THE FINEST WINES, LIQUORS AND CIGARS
A Splendid Lunch Every Day at 11 A. M.

CITY DIRECTORY ADS 1866
The year after the war ended advertising reflected a variety of mercantile offerings by new and old businesses.

John Dawson married Eugene Magevney's daughter Kate in 1867 at St. Peter's Catholic Church, next door to the Magevney home. Kate was the first cousin of Dawson's former commander, Michael Magevney. Benedict Joseph Semmes was scouring Europe for select vintages to restock his store of fine wines and liquors while his first cousin Raphael, the former Confederate admiral and commander of the *Alabama*, was now the editor of a Memphis newspaper, the *Bulletin*.

Another former Confederate soldier, the French emigré John Gaston, opened his Commercial Restaurant on Adams near Main. The excellence of his cuisine was attracting gentlemen for a la carte breakfasts, lunches and suppers in such numbers that Gaston was preparing to move to larger quarters and open the Gaston Hotel. Confederate engineering officer Minor Meriwether was back at work as a civil engineer for the railroad.

Forrest had returned to farm his Mississippi plan-

NATHAN BEDFORD FORREST
After the war Forrest was an aging man, troubled by ill health and financial reverses that prevented him from recouping the large fortune lost in supporting the South.

B. J. SEMMES
Benedict Joseph Semmes served in the 154th Senior Tennessee Infantry Regiment as sergeant of Company L and was wounded at Shiloh and Atlanta. Promoted to captain, Semmes was paroled at Gainesville, Alabama, with the troops of General Forrest. After the war he and one of his former commanders, Lieutenant Colonel John Dawson (Kate Magevney's husband), reestablished his wholesale wine and liquor business.

tation at Sunflower Landing after the war. He also engaged in other businesses, including the Memphis & Selma Railroad and an insurance company, to help him regain the $1,500,000 he had lost through his support of the Confederate cause. Both the insurance company and the railroad venture failed, hard hit by the chaotic postwar financial conditions, and in 1868 Forrest declared bankruptcy. Devotion to the former "Wizard of the Saddle," who had pledged his life and fortune to the Confederacy, was not diminished by peace. When the bankruptcy proceedings opened, no creditors put in an appearance.

Perhaps the strongest evidence of the rebirth of Memphis came in the winter of 1869, with the opening of the Peabody House at Main and Monroe. Architect for this new hotel was Edward Culliatt Jones, who had come to Memphis from Charleston, South Carolina, in 1866. He was hired by Robert Campbell Brinkley to remodel the Brinkley Block of seven stores on the northwest corner of Main and Monroe into a five-story structure, originally to be called the Brinkley House.

Brinkley had married the daughter of John Overton, one of Memphis' original proprietors, and had moved to Memphis to supervise his father-in-law's large property interests. While in Europe to purchase railroad track for the Memphis & Charleston, Brinkley made the acquaintance of an English banker, George Peabody, and the friendship which developed between the two men continued throughout their lives. Shortly before the opening of the hotel on February 5, 1869, Brinkley received news of his friend's death and renamed the building the Peabody House in his honor.

The new hotel was launched with a glittering ball attended by 200 guests. This event was the birth of what was to become a Mid-South tradition and was described by the *Daily Post* the following day in glowing detail:

"Mine generous hosts Cockrell and sons of the Peabody Hotel gave a grand ball to their patrons and guests

ROBERT BRINKLEY
Brinkley was one of the few prominent Memphians who lived through the war and occupation years with his fortune relatively intact. He was a leading promoter of railroads both before and after the Civil War. One of his former work camp stations in Arkansas bears his name today.

TENNESSEE – THE PEABODY HOUSE IN MEMPHIS.
(Reproduced from the original print in the collections of the Memphis Pink Palace Museum.)

last night which again fulfilled their long-standing reputation of being the champions in all matters relating to dancing and feasting. Every member of the brilliant throng which graced the spacious and elegant hall last night was . . . sure of an unbounded enjoyment. . . . "

A preview of this "hostelry of hospitality" had been given in early December, even before the finishing touches had been completed on the building. A fancy masked ball began at 10 o'clock with partygoers in "gay and elegant dress, representing dead kings, heroes, heroines, fairies, goddesses, nuns, clowns and everything else you could imagine."

The Peabody, which was built at a cost of $60,000, contained 75 rooms with private baths, a ballroom, a

1868 FASHION
(*Sketched from* Harper's Bazar)

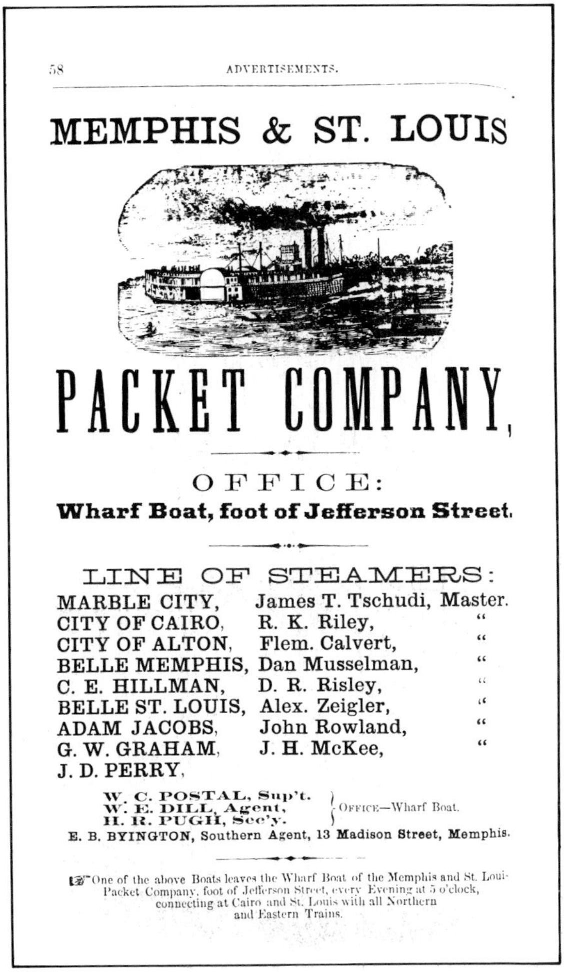
58 ADVERTISEMENTS.

MEMPHIS & ST. LOUIS

PACKET COMPANY,

OFFICE:

Wharf Boat, foot of Jefferson Street.

LINE OF STEAMERS:

MARBLE CITY,	James T. Tschudi, Master.
CITY OF CAIRO,	R. K. Riley, "
CITY OF ALTON,	Flem. Calvert, "
BELLE MEMPHIS,	Dan Musselman, "
C. E. HILLMAN,	D. R. Risley, "
BELLE ST. LOUIS,	Alex. Zeigler, "
ADAM JACOBS,	John Rowland, "
G. W. GRAHAM,	J. H. McKee, "
J. D. PERRY,	

W. C. POSTAL, Sup't.
W. E. DILL, Agent, } OFFICE—Wharf Boat.
H. R. PUGH, Sec'y.

E. B. BYINGTON, Southern Agent, 13 Madison Street, Memphis.

☞ One of the above Boats leaves the Wharf Boat of the Memphis and St. Loui- Packet Company, foot of Jefferson Street, every Evening at 5 o'clock, connecting at Cairo and St. Louis with all Northern and Eastern Trains.

MEMPHIS – ST. LOUIS PACKET CO. Many packet companies were operating lines out of Memphis during the postwar years to capitalize on the passenger and freight river traffic.

saloon, lobby and a dining room and kitchen on the same floor (an innovation for that day). Meals were included in the $4-a-day room price, but there was an extra charge for gas lights and a fire in the fireplace. In the Peabody Concert Saloon and the Billiard Parlor, mint juleps, bourbon and other liquors were served by bartender Ben Hollander. The Peabody's Saloon became the special target for reformers, because the "ladies" gathered for the beer and music were not ladies at all, but "seductive sirens" hoping to obtain money from an unwary traveler by any means possible.

Later in 1869 Robert Brinkley gave the Peabody as

a wedding gift to his daughter, Annie Overton Brinkley, on the occasion of her marriage to Robert Bogardus Snowden. Until 1923, when the old hotel was replaced by the Lowenstein building, the Snowden family was connected with the affairs of the Peabody.

In early July 1870 crowds gathered in the lobby of the Peabody to learn the latest news of the great river race between the *Natchez* and the *Robert E. Lee* as they steamed upstream from New Orleans to St. Louis. Betting on arrival times at different river ports became heavy as the telegraph dispatches were received and posted. Vicksburg reported to the editors of the *Appeal* that the *Robert E. Lee* had passed the foot of Crawford Street at "5." A Vicksburg correspondent reported to the *Appeal* at 8:10 A.M. on July 2 that Captain Cannon's *Robert E. Lee* was then 14 to 16 minutes ahead but that Captain Leathers' *Natchez* was making good time in spite of stops for passengers and freight.

As the two great steamboats moved toward Memphis, the excitement mounted. At 2 P.M., a dispatch from Vicksburg announced that the *Lee* was 45 minutes ahead at Lake Washington, 100 miles above Vicksburg, but that when the *Natchez* passed the same point, it had been moving very fast. Also at 2 P.M. coal merchants Brown and Jones received a telegram in Memphis to have coal flats ready for the *Lee* at 7 o'clock.

From Helena, Arkansas, came the report that "the *R. E. Lee* passed up at 4:30 and the *Natchez* at 5:24" headed for Memphis, and this news from the telegraph office spread throughout the city. By 10 o'clock that evening an estimated 20,000 persons packed the river landing, the bluffs, galleries and housetops fronting the river, watching for the first of the racers to make its appearance. A few minutes before 11 P.M. the *Lee* rounded the point below the city and landed amid cheers and wild excitement. She lost one minute at the landing, probably two more in making her coal barges fast as she

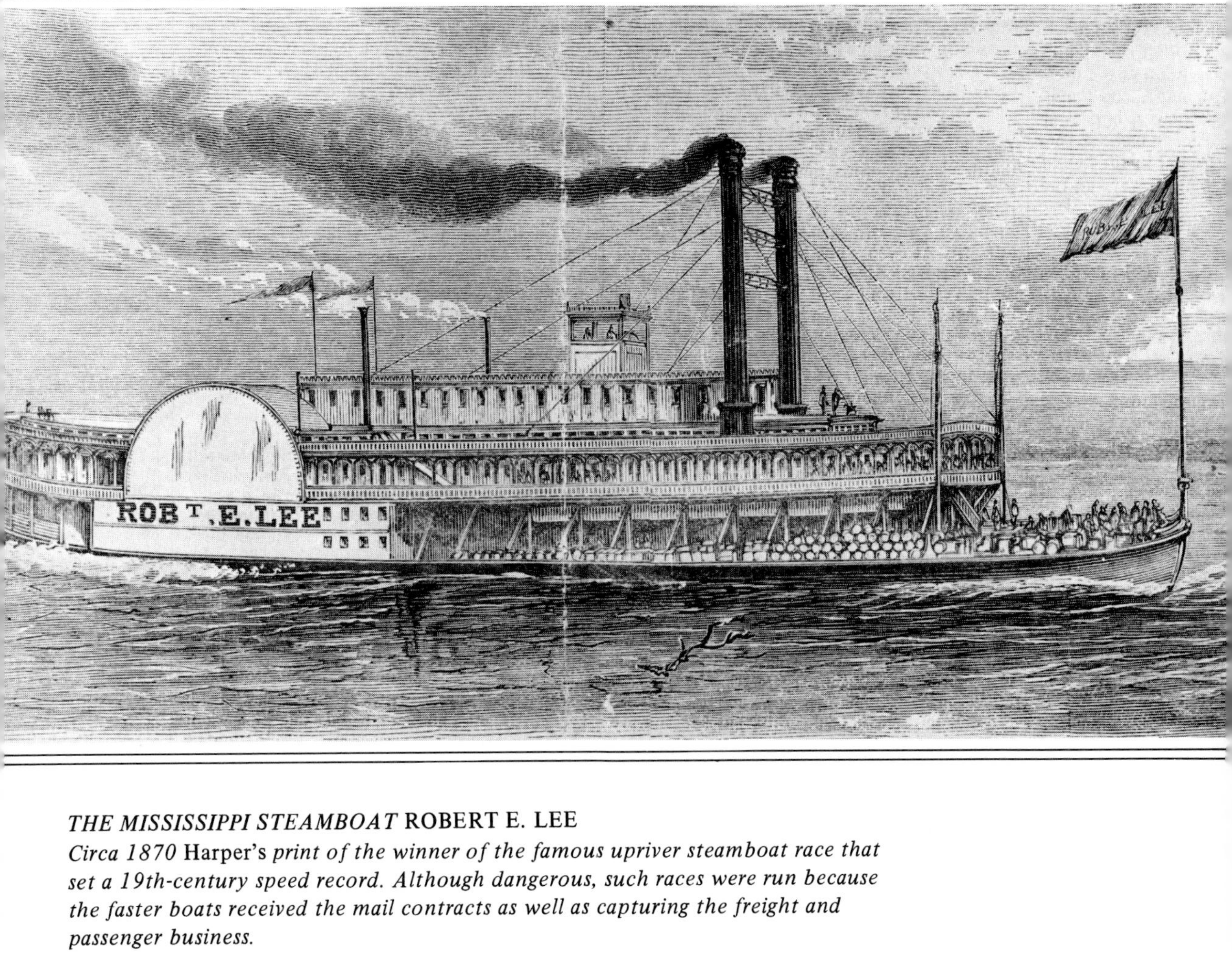

THE MISSISSIPPI STEAMBOAT ROBERT E. LEE
Circa 1870 Harper's *print of the winner of the famous upriver steamboat race that set a 19th-century speed record. Although dangerous, such races were run because the faster boats received the mail contracts as well as capturing the freight and passenger business.*

turned upstream. At 12:13 A.M., one hour and three minutes behind the *Lee*, the *Natchez* rounded the Arkansas point and picked up her coal barges. Between Cairo and St. Louis a heavy fog came down, but the *Lee* refused to stop because the *Natchez* was making up lost time and beginning to gain. Captain Leathers ordered the *Natchez* to anchor for the safety of his boat and cargo until the pilot could see ahead.

The whole of St. Louis turned out to welcome the *Robert E. Lee* when it pulled up to the landing at 11:25 on the morning of July 4, three days, 18 hours and 14 minutes after leaving New Orleans. It was the greatest race ever run on the Father of Waters. Although that record would be beaten many times in coming years, it became known as *the* race of the century. All bets were paid by the losers, but old-time rivermen still claimed the *Natchez* to be the faster boat. It was just that Captain Leathers would never let a boat of his do anything to discredit the name "Robert E. Lee."

Three months later Memphians mourned the death of that beloved leader of the Confederate army. The local tribute, as reported by the *Avalanche*, was not confined by class or sectionalism as a symbolic funeral ceremony was carried out:

" . . . Scarcely a building on the long line of the funeral procession was without a mark of respect to the lamented dead. Citizens who had worn the gray; those who had worn the blue; Federal and Confederate; forgetting the terrible scenes of other days and ignoring the past, joined in this last sad tribute. . . . "

The marchers carried both Federal and Confederate flags down Main Street so thronged with spectators they could hardly pass. The City Band under Professor J. G. Handwerker played a solemn dirge as it followed the guard of honor, the De Soto Guards, at a funeral pace. General Lee had been an honorary member of this company. At Court Square a huge crowd had gathered to

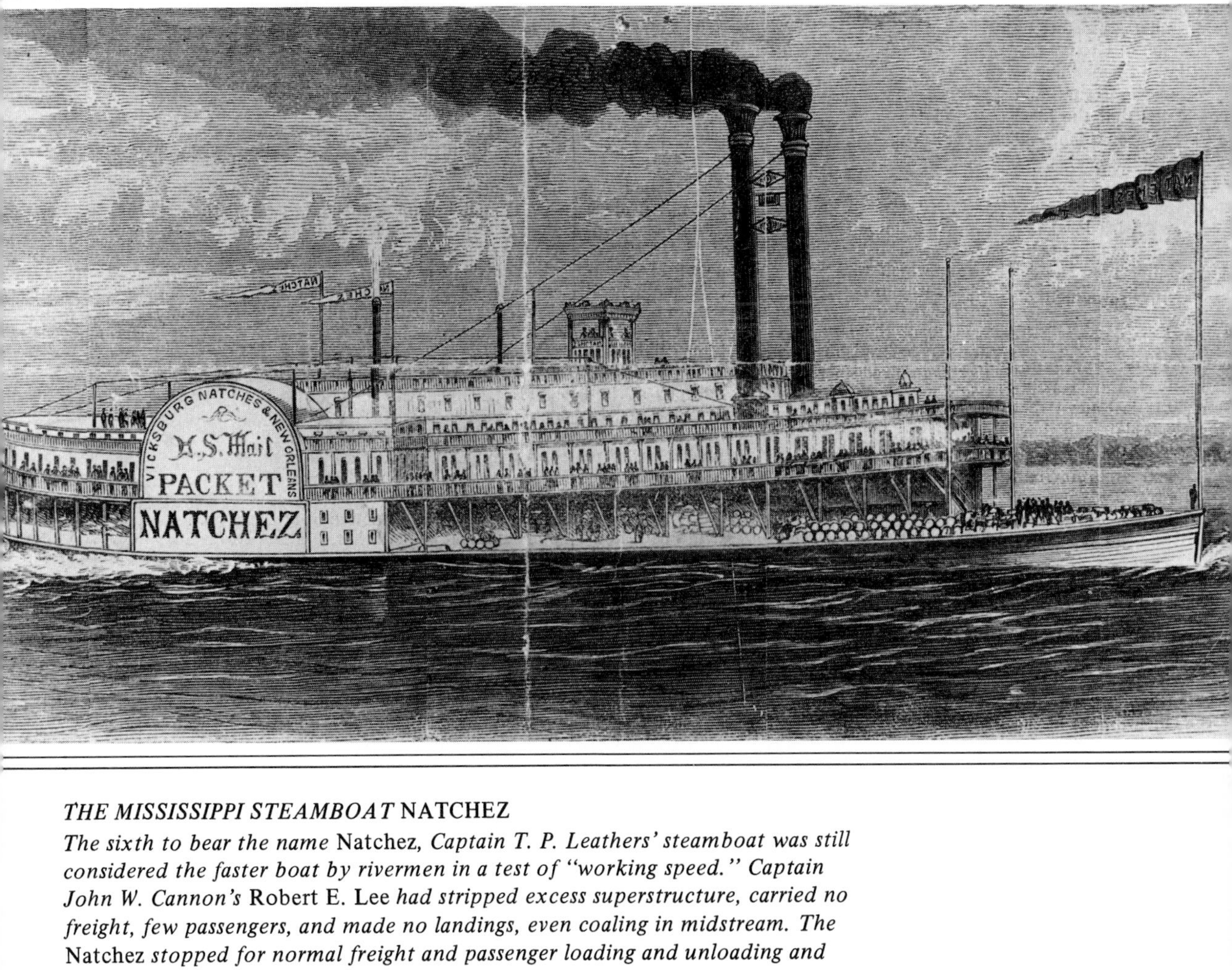

THE MISSISSIPPI STEAMBOAT NATCHEZ

The sixth to bear the name Natchez, *Captain T. P. Leathers' steamboat was still considered the faster boat by rivermen in a test of "working speed." Captain John W. Cannon's* Robert E. Lee *had stripped excess superstructure, carried no freight, few passengers, and made no landings, even coaling in midstream. The* Natchez *stopped for normal freight and passenger loading and unloading and waited out a fog for almost five hours while the* Lee *raced on to St. Louis.*

CONFEDERATE VETERAN'S UNIFORM
The United Confederate Veterans was organized after the war to assist disabled comrades, destitute widows and orphans. Its Northern counterpart was the Grand Army of the Republic.

watch as the death symbol, an empty coffin, was borne from the hearse and into the square, where it was placed within the enclosure behind Andrew Jackson's statue.

For those close enough to see, the words of the battered inscription on the pedestal's north side were a stark reminder of the past:

> THE FEDERAL UNION: IT MUST AND SHALL BE PRESERVED.

Old Hickory could now rest; the fragmented Union was whole again.

For the blacks of Memphis and ethnic immigrant minorities, opportunities to succeed would come in the next decades. As leaders and innovators they would be a part of a general mood of recovery, growth and optimism, indicative of a still explosively growing America. None could conceive of the truly tragic times that would come to Memphis within a few years. How could a city that had sacrificed so many sons to a lost cause and suffered the indignation of three years of occupation by a victorious enemy be hurt again? No one understood that the irritating stings of mosquitoes could bring death in epidemic proportions and total financial ruin for a city. The worst was yet to come.

HANDBLOWN GLASS VASES
This 1860's pair of "Mary Gregory" design vases are of lime-green tinted handblown glass. Each vase has a bulbous base with a flared top and is decorated with a white figure. At left is a young girl holding a flower in an extended hand and on the right a boy also holding a flower.

Selected Bibliography

Amann, William Frayne, editor. *Personnel of the Civil War.* Two Volumes. New York and London: Thomas Yoseloff, Publisher, 1961.

Campbell, Robert A. *The Rebellion Register.* Indianapolis, Indiana: A. D. Streight Publisher, 1867.

Capers, Gerald M., Jr. *The Biography of a River Town.* Second Edition. Tulane University: Gerald M. Capers, Jr., 1966.

Catton, Bruce. *This Hallowed Ground.* New York: Pocket Books, 1956.

Church, Annette E. and Roberta. *The Robert R. Churches of Memphis.* Ann Arbor, Michigan: Edwards Brothers Printers, 1974.

Coggins, Jack. *Arms and Equipment of the Civil War.* Garden City, New York: Doubleday & Company, Inc., 1962.

Connelley, Thomas L. *Civil War Tennessee: Battles and Leaders.* Knoxville, Tennessee: The University of Tennessee Press, 1979.

Coppock, Paul R. *Memphis Sketches.* Memphis: Friends of Memphis and Shelby County Libraries, 1976.

Cortese, James, editor. *The Bluff City, A Newspaper History.* Moweaqua, Illinois: Spectator Books, 1978.

Goodspeed. *History of Hamilton, Knox and Shelby Counties of Tennessee.* Nashville: Goodspeed Publishing Company, 1887. Reprinted Nashville: Charles and Randy Elder, Booksellers, 1974.

Henry, Robert Selph, editor. *As They Saw Forrest.* Jackson, Tennessee: McCowat-Mercer Press, Inc., 1956.

Henry, Robert Selph. *"First With the Most": Forrest.* Jackson, Tennessee: McCowat-Mercer Press, Inc., 1944.

Horn, Stanley F. *The Army of Tennessee.* Norman, Oklahoma: University of Oklahoma Press, 1952.

Horn, Stanley F., Editor. *Tennessee's War 1861–1865: Described by Participants.* Nashville, Tennessee: Tennessee Civil War Centennial Commission, 1965.

Jordan, General Thomas and Pryor, J. P. *The Campaigns of Lieut.-Gen. N. B. Forrest and of Forrest's Cavalry.* Dayton, Ohio: Press of Morningside Bookshop, 1973.

Jordan, Robert Paul. *The Civil War.* New York: The National Geographic Society, 1969.

Keating, John M. *History of the City of Memphis and Shelby County.* Two Volumes. Syracuse, New York: D. Mason & Co., Publishers, 1888.

Lord, Francis A. *Civil War Collector's Encyclopedia.* Harrisburg, Pennsylvania: The Stackpole Company, 1963.

Meriwether, Elizabeth Avery. *Recollections of 92 Years 1824–1916.* Nashville, Tennessee: The Tennessee Historical Commission, 1958.

Miller, Francis Trevelyan, editor. *The Photographic History of the Civil War.* 10 Volumes. New York and London: Thomas Yoseloff, 1957.

Robertson, James I., Jr. *The Concise Illustrated History of the Civil War.* Gettysburg, Pennsylvania: The National Historical Society, 1971.

Sigafoos, Robert A. *Cotton Row to Beale Street.* Memphis: Memphis State University Press, 1979.

The West Tennessee Historical Society Papers. Memphis: The West Tennessee Historical Society.

Warner, Ezra J. *Generals in Blue.* Baton Rouge, Louisiana: Louisiana State University Press, 1964.

Warner, Ezra J. *Generals in Gray.* Baton Rouge, Louisiana: Louisiana State University Press, 1959.

Young, Judge J. P. *Standard History of Memphis, Tennessee.* Knoxville, Tennessee: H. W. Crew & Co., 1912.

List of Illustrations

Chapter 4

Conquered City

Chapter 5

An Impoverished Peace

Chapter 6

Rebuilding a City

The Historic Counties of West Tennessee

BENTON: Created 1836. Named for early settler, David Benton; Seat, Camden.

CARROLL: Created 1821. Named for Tennessee Governor William Carroll; Seat, Huntingdon.

CHESTER: Created 1879. Named for Colonel Robert Chester (War of 1812); Seat, Henderson.

CROCKETT: Created 1871. Named for frontiersman and congressman "Davy" Crockett; Seat, Alamo.

DECATUR: Created 1845. Named for Commodore Stephen Decatur (Tripolitanian War); Seat, Decaturville.

DYER: Created 1823. Named for Colonel Robert Henry Dyer (War of 1812 and Indian wars); Seat, Dyersburg.

FAYETTE: Created 1824. Named for Marquis de LaFayette, French hero of the American Revolution; Seat, Somerville.

GIBSON: Created 1823. Named for Colonel John Gibson (Creek Wars and Natchez Expedition); Seat, Trenton.

HARDEMAN: Created in 1823. Named for Colonel Thomas Jones Hardeman (War of 1812); Seat, Bolivar.

HARDIN: Created 1819. Named for Colonel Joseph Hardin (Revolutionary War); Seat, Savannah.

HAYWOOD: Created in 1823. Named for Tennessee Supreme Court Justice John Haywood; Seat, Brownsville.

HENDERSON: Created 1821. Named for Colonel James Henderson (War of 1812); Seat, Lexington.

HENRY: Created 1821. Named for Revolutionary War patriot and Virginia governor Patrick Henry; Seat, Paris.

LAKE: Created 1870. Named for Reelfoot Lake; Seat, Tiptonville.

LAUDERDALE: Created 1835. Named for Colonel James Lauderdale (War of 1812); Seat, Ripley.

McNAIRY: Created 1823. Named for Judge John McNairy, early federal judge; Seat, Selmer.

MADISON: Created 1821. Named for President James Madison; Seat, Jackson.

OBION: Created 1823. Named for the Obion River; Seat, Union City.

SHELBY: Created 1819. Named for Governor Isaac Shelby of Kentucky who helped negotiate the opening of West Tennessee to settlement; Seat, Memphis.

TIPTON: Created 1823. Named for Jacob Tipton, killed in early Indian War; Seat, Covington.

WEAKLEY: Created 1823. Named for Robert Weakley, early Tennessee settler: Seat, Dresden.

ABOUT THE MEMPHIS PINK PALACE MUSEUM

THE ORIGINAL "Pink Palace" building was constructed in the late 1920's as the mansion of multimillionaire Clarence Saunders, inventor of the self-service grocery story. After Saunders lost his fortune on the New York Stock Exchange, the 160 acre estate was bought by real estate developers, and the unfinished mansion was given to the city for a museum. Although initially named the Memphis Museum of Natural History and Industrial Arts, the public promptly dubbed it the "Pink Palace" because of the exterior of rose-colored Georgian marble. Today exhibits and collections are housed in a large modern addition while classrooms, laboratories, meeting rooms and administrative offices are situated in the old "Pink Palace" mansion.